THIS BOOK BELONGS TO:

....

....

T0012671

www.rebelgirls.com

Library of Congress Control Number: 2023945392
Rebel Girls, Inc.
421 Elm Ave.
Larkspur, CA 94939

Text by Michelle Schusterman and Cara Goodwin
Art direction by Giulia Flamini
Cover illustrations by Julia Christians
Graphic design by Kristen Brittain
Editor: Jess Harriton
Special thanks: Eliza Kirby, Hannah Bennett, Jes Wolfe, Sarah Parvis

Printed in China, 2024
10 9 8 7 6 5 4 3 2 1
ISBN: 979-8-88964-100-1

CONTENTS

Chapter 3:
Communication Is Key 61

Chapter 4:
Sticky Situations 82

Chapter 5:
Tough Stuff 108

Chapter 6:
You've Got This! 130

Scan the QR code to unlock more confidence-boosting content on the Rebel Girls app. Listeners will celebrate the messiness of growing up with game shows, mindfulness breaks, advice from experts, and more!

INTRODUCTION

Hi there, Rebels!

Welcome to *Growing Up Powerful: Social Situation Survival Guide.* We're thrilled you're here. Maybe you're already familiar with this series, or our Good Night Stories series, or our podcast. Or perhaps the title of this book caught your eye, and you thought: *wait, there's a guidebook to social situations? Sign me up!*

As you grow up, you'll be presented with all kinds of exciting opportunities: making friends, discovering what you love to do, and learning new things. You're going to find hobbies and passions and form relationships. You'll become more independent and develop a stronger sense of self while also figuring out what role you want to play in your community (and the world!). All of these experiences help shape you into the clever, curious, kind Rebel Girl that you are.

But sometimes, these joyful milestones come with challenges. Certain social situations can feel like navigating a maze. How do you strike up a conversation with someone new at school or camp? What should you do when you see someone being bullied? How do you help a friend who is going through a tough time?

Do you worry about introducing yourself when you're the new kid in a group? Check out our tips on page 11. Wondering what to do when you have a super cringey moment? Turn to page 83 for advice on how to get past it. Just found out your best friend is moving away, and you are having a hard time? We've got your back on page 121. Struggling with anxiety anytime you hear the news or when you're confronted with serious issues in your community? Flip to page 143, and we'll walk you through it. Have a crush on someone and have no clue how to handle it? Page 49 has you covered, and we'll talk about what to do when someone has a crush on you too.

And it's not just advice! This guidebook is loaded with fun quizzes on topics like where to look for new friends, how to stand up for yourself, and figuring out what positive changes you can make in the world. There are also lots of stories and quotes from Rebel Girls just like you who get anxious in social situations.

Socializing can be overwhelming. But it can also be fun. In the meantime, we're here for you at this awesome time in your life filled with new friends and exciting experiences. With this book, you'll feel ready to handle any challenge that comes your way—the good, the bad, and the totally awkward!

Stay Rebel!
The Rebel Girls Team

CHAPTER 1

CONVERSATION 101

Look over there! See that girl waving at you across the street? She looks really familiar. You know her from school, right? Or wait, maybe she was in that dance class you took last summer. Ack, she's coming over! Did she just move here? Maybe you don't know her at all, and she just wants to meet a new neighbor. Or maybe she was that girl you met at the coding club competition a few months ago and she'll be hurt if you don't remember her name, and now she's standing right in front of you, and—*Come on, brain, how do I say hi?*

It's a simple word, but it can cause us to feel BIG anxiety—because hi is usually followed by more talking. From introducing yourself to your new classmates to making small talk with a neighbor in the elevator, we're going to cover all the basics in this chapter so you feel like a conversational wizard.

HOW TO INTRODUCE YOURSELF WHEN YOU'RE THE NEW KID

Being the new kid can be super scary. The school might look like a maze, you don't know any of the teachers, and of course, it seems like all the other students have been friends since kindergarten. How do you fit in? What if you don't make any friends at all?

And it's not just school. What about summer camp? Joining a club or an extracurricular like theater or band? Volunteering at an animal shelter with a bunch of kids you've never met before?

Before you spiral, take a deep breath—and give yourself a break. Pretty much no one makes a tight-knit group of friends on the very first day of school, camp, or any other activity. Making friends takes time!

But there are definitely a few things you can do to get off on the right foot when you introduce yourself.

Try these tactics:

* **Smile!** Chances are, you aren't the only one who's anxious. A smile makes others feel at ease and welcomes them to talk to you.

* **Say your name.** A simple "Hi, I'm Gemma" will do—and make sure to pause so they have time to give you their names.

* **Ask a question.** If you just say hi, the dreaded awkward silence might follow. Questions invite conversation, and as a new kid to the party, you've probably got plenty: "Where's the gym?" "Who's the nicest camp counselor?" "How long have you been a volunteer?"

* **Pay attention.** Sometimes, we're so nervous that we blurt out a question then don't listen to the response. Make sure you listen when the other person is talking so you can keep the conversation going.

HOW TO MAKE A PHONE CALL

Does the idea of calling someone fill you with dread? It's not just you! A lot of people feel awkward on the phone. Plus, texting is so much easier!

But texting isn't always an option. And not all restaurants offer online ordering. You might have to call the salon to make an appointment to get your nails done, or ask a pet supply store how late they're open, or find out if a bakery has vegan options. Sometimes, a phone call is your only choice . . . and that's okay.

A few minutes of preparation before you dial is all you need if you're feeling overwhelmed.

*   **Take notes.** First, take a few notes on why you're calling. For example, if you're ordering food, write down your exact order in case your mind goes blank during the call. Having your notes at hand will help you relax.

*   **Avoid background noise.** Make sure you're in a quiet area or room before you make the call. Let any nearby family members or friends know you're going to be on the phone so they won't interrupt you.

*   **Speak clearly and politely.** No matter who you're calling, it's a good idea to talk as you would to a teacher rather than your bestie. ("Hello, this is Jackie," not "Hey, what's up?") If you're calling to chat with a specific person, ask for them by name and be sure to state your own. ("Hi, this is Amy. Is Sabrina there?") If you're calling for another reason, like ordering food or asking about business hours, there's no need to introduce yourself in your greeting. ("Good morning! I was wondering what time the library closes today.")

*   **Talk slower than usual.** You might have noticed it's a little more difficult to understand someone when you can't see their lips move.

* **Say thank you.** At the end of the conversation, thank them for their time. Don't forget to say goodbye before you hang up!

* **Leave a message.** If you make a call and it goes straight to voicemail, don't panic! Introduce yourself, explain why you're calling (using your handy notes if you need them), and make sure to leave the best phone number for them to return your call.

HOW TO ORDER AT A RESTAURANT

You're sitting at a long table with your volleyball teammates after a match. Everyone's laughing and talking, and the restaurant is pretty crowded too. Suddenly, the waiter is right next to your chair. "Can I take your order?"

Eek! Your brain jams, and your mouth opens but no words come out. Ordering food at a restaurant can be intimidating. When you were little, an adult at the table probably told the waiter what you wanted. But now it's time for you to order for yourself. If talking with a waiter makes you feel a little anxious, just keep the following tips in mind when you go out to eat.

- ✳ **Look at the menu first.** Going out to eat is a fun social occasion, and it's easy to get caught up in conversation with everyone at the table. Make sure you read the menu when you get to the restaurant so you know what you want when the waiter arrives. If you know where you are going ahead of time, you can even take a peek at the menu before you get there.

- ✳ **Greet the waiter.** It's more polite than simply launching into your order. A simple hi will do the trick!

- ✳ **Speak slowly and clearly.** Restaurants can be noisy, with lots of chatter and the clatter of dishes. Look at your waiter and speak up to make sure they can hear you.

- ✳ **Have your menu handy.** If you freeze up, no worries! Just point to the menu item you want.

- ✳ **Say thank you.** Sometimes, service workers have to deal with rude customers. A thank you and a smile can show appreciation and help brighten their day.

WHAT IS MY BODY SAYING?

Obviously, conversations are made up of words. But while your mouth is talking, the rest of your body is communicating too—even if you don't realize it.

Imagine telling a friend that you lost the necklace she let you borrow. After you apologize, she puts a hand on your arm and says, "Don't worry about it!" with a bright smile. You're probably pretty relieved she isn't mad.

But what if she mumbles, "Don't worry about it" while crossing her arms and staring at the ground? Uh-oh. Something tells you that you *should* be worried about it. Because despite what she's saying, her body language is making it pretty clear she's upset.

Body language can be conscious, which basically means we're doing it on purpose. When you stand up and cheer at a softball game because someone hit a home run, you're using your body language to show how happy and excited you are. But body language can be unconscious too.

When your crush walks past your locker, you might blush, fidget, and grin without even realizing it. You didn't call out, "Hey, I have a crush on you!" but your body language is sure trying to communicate that.

Body language includes . . .

✳ **Facial expressions.** Smiling, frowning, rolling your eyes, wrinkling your nose . . . these all communicate very different messages.

✳ **Posture.** Are you holding your head high, or tucking your chin to your neck? Crossing your arms, or clasping your hands behind your back?

✳ **Gestures.** The more emotional we are, the more we tend to move our hands and arms. You might wave your hands when you're excited, or ball your hands into fists when you're angry.

* **Eye contact.** It's difficult for many people to hide their emotions, because our eyes tend to give away exactly how we're feeling. And some people, including many neurodivergent people, find making eye contact uncomfortable.

* **Touch.** Hugs, high fives, pats on the back—how you touch someone can tell them a lot.

* **Tone.** How many different ways can you say the word *yes*? Excited, confused, upset, sad, afraid, sarcastic . . . the tone of your voice says just as much as your words.

Strike a Superhero Pose!

Consciously adjusting your body language can change your feelings and self-perception. When we're nervous, our bodies tend to "shrink." If we're hunching our shoulders or bowing our heads, our bodies are telling the world, "Please don't look at me—I'm super nervous right now!"

Let's say you have to do a presentation in front of your class, or it's your first day on the swim team—basically anything that makes you feel a little bit anxious. All you want is to be cool and confident. Who's more confident than a superhero?

Try this: stand in front of a mirror and strike a superhero pose. Plant your feet firmly on the floor shoulder-width apart, place your hands on your hips with your elbows jutting out, lift your chin high—and smile. Stay in this position for five minutes. It might feel a little silly, but studies show that the superhero pose can help you feel more confident.

Penny has always been shy. She never raises her hand when the teacher asks a question, even if she knows the answer. She'd much rather watch movies with a few close friends than go to a big party where she probably won't know everyone. And while she loves playing tennis on the weekends for fun, the idea of playing a match in front of a crowd makes her legs wobble.

So when Penny's parents send her to summer camp, all she can think is: *this is a nightmare!*

Penny hugs her duffel bag and tennis racket as she steps off the bus. The campground is swarming with kids, and her stomach is doing flip-flops. There's lots of talking and laughing and hugging as girls reunite with the friends they made last summer, and Penny hangs off to the side. She wants to make new friends, but it's so hard.

The counselors start handing out ice pops. One of them spots Penny watching the other campers chatting and giggling as they gather around the coolers. "Try this," the counselor says with a wink. "Just pick someone who looks friendly and smile at them. That's it!"

Penny gulps nervously and nods. She looks around until she spots a camper carrying a backpack—and a tennis racket.

Her heart lifts, and she waits until the girl glances up and sees her. Penny smiles. The girl smiles back . . . and walks over.

"Hi! I'm Heather," she says. "Want to come get an ice pop?"

"Okay!" Penny can't stop smiling as Heather starts talking about her favorite tennis players. Maybe summer camp won't be so bad after all.

SMALL TALK CAN FEEL LIKE A BIG DEAL

You step into the empty elevator in your apartment building and press 12. But just as the doors slide closed, someone sticks their arm in to open them again. It's a girl whose aunt lives next to you—and now you're stuck in the elevator together. For. Twelve. Whole. Floors.

What are you going to talk about?

Standing in total silence can feel super awkward. That's why "small talk" is considered a valuable social skill. Small talk is light, informal chitchat about things everyone has an opinion on, like the weather, the latest movies, or favorite foods. If making small talk with a stranger—or even with someone you kinda sorta know—makes you nervous, you're not alone. But studies show that it is good for our mental well-being. According to an article in *Discover* magazine, "Building rapport with strangers can leave people feeling heard, respected, and emotionally validated." That's right: spending a few minutes chatting about K-pop with that girl in the elevator might start off feeling uncomfortable, but by the end, you're likely to be in a better mood. Who knows—you might even have a new friend!

But seriously, what are you going to talk about?

Here are a few small-talk tips for different situations:

* ✳ **Compliments are great.** While it's not the best idea to comment on someone's body (even in a nice way), complimenting things like clothes or jewelry can be a great icebreaker. Is she carrying a book you've read? Wearing the T-shirt of a band you love?

* ✳ **Context can help.** Your surroundings and current situation give you and the other person automatic things in common. For example, if you're

in the orthodontist's waiting room with another patient, you might make small talk about your experience with braces so far.

✳ **Ask and answer.** Simple questions like, "How was your weekend?" can get the conversation going. Make sure when it's your turn to answer, you go beyond a simple yes and no and open up a little! For example, if someone asks you how your summer break is going, don't just say "fine." Tell her about your trip to visit your cousins or all the time you spent at the community pool.

What's Your Social Situation Comfort Level?

1. Your birthday's coming up! What's the perfect way to celebrate?

A. What else? PARTY! An epic blowout with all my friends! Dancing, food, karaoke . . . Ooh, is there a concert we could all go to together?!

B. Something fun with a tight group of friends, like bowling or laser tag. And we could all go out for ice cream afterwards.

C. Invite my friends over for a board game night, or maybe a slumber party. We could order pizza and eat birthday cake.

D. Just me and my bestie binging Netflix rom-coms with a giant bowl of popcorn and cupcakes from my favorite bakery.

2. You had a stressful week at school: a new group project, a big track meet, and a brutal social studies test. Now it's finally the weekend. What's your plan?

A. Rallying as many of my friends as I can to meet up. We might spend all day at the mall shopping, catch a movie, or even hit the ice skating rink.

B. My best friend is on the softball team, and they have a game. I'll go cheer her on—that's a good way to vent some stress!

C. My favorite way to decompress is having a few friends over to bake cookies and listen to music.

D. Just give me a blanket, a book, and a mug of hot chocolate.

3. If your friends picked your perfect career, what would they probably say?

A. Anything that puts me in the spotlight: pop star, actress, politician, TikTok sensation . . .

B. Maybe a teacher or a doctor? Something that lets me work with lots of people.
C. Probably a job that calls for teamwork, like a lab scientist or publishing or social media management.
D. Something that lets me work in peace and quiet, like writing, graphic design, or coding.

4. **You just had a disagreement with a friend, and now things are totally awkward between you. The next time you see her, you . . .**

A. Walk up to her and address the issue. There's no sense letting things get even more awkward.
B. Break the ice with a joke and see how she reacts.
C. Catch her eye and wave, but wait a little bit before talking about it.
D. Wonder if there is a closet I can hide in until she's gone?!

5. **After a few weeks of art class, you've finished your first painting. It's not perfect, but you're really proud of your accomplishment. You . . .**

A. Snap a photo and share it online with every hashtag imaginable.
B. See what my teacher and classmates think of it first, then show my friends and family.
C. Give it to a friend or loved one as a gift.
D. Smuggle it home and put it in my room—someplace out of sight.

6. **A new friend invites you to a meetup at a pizza place. When you get there, she hasn't arrived . . . but the other kids, who you don't know yet, are already at a table. What do you do?**

A. Join the fun!
B. Wait for a break in the conversation, then introduce myself.
C. Text my friend to see how close she is, then hang outside and wait for her.
D. Turn around and leave. I can order pizza at home.

7. **It's summer break, and your friends are all away on vacation. Your parents are at work, so it's only you at home. How are you feeling?**

   A. Bored, bored, and bored.
   B. A little antsy . . . I might take a walk around my neighborhood.
   C. Pretty relaxed. I'm sitting in the backyard listening to my favorite podcast with a glass of lemonade, or maybe doing a little gaming.
   D. Are you kidding? I'm living my best life with the house all to myself!

Answers

Mostly As: Social Butterfly

There's no doubt about it—you thrive on social interactions. It's awesome that you feel so comfortable in so many social situations. Just make sure you're giving your friends as much attention and adoration as they're showing you.

Mostly Bs: Low-Key Extrovert

You're a people person, for sure. It's pretty easy for you to make new friends, and of course, you've got your regular squad too. Remember, if you ever feel like you need a little "me time," that's completely okay! There's nothing wrong with taking the occasional day to decompress by yourself.

Mostly Cs: Super Chill

You're comfortable with being on your own, and that's fantastic! It's great to have solo interests and passions. But don't let your anxiety keep you from accepting invitations to hang out with the group if you really want to. Your nerves will disappear after a few minutes, and you'll end up having a great time.

Mostly Ds: Queen of Quiet

You know what you're about: you! It's seriously so cool that you're content hanging out on your own—as long as you're doing it because you want to and not because you're afraid. If you think you're dealing with social anxiety, remember, you're not alone! Try hanging out with one or two friends a few times a week to ease yourself into it.

ASK THE EXPERT

Cara Goodwin, PhD
Child Psychologist

How can I be more confident about raising
my hand in class?
–Chase, 11, Colorado, USA

Speaking up in class can be intimidating, so it's completely normal to feel nervous about it. However, it is really important to remember that the more you do it, the easier it will get. When you feel nervous about something and you avoid it, your anxiety tends to get worse over time. On the other hand, if you face your fears and do it even though you're nervous, it will get easier and easier. But don't worry—you don't have to raise your hand in your toughest class first thing tomorrow! You can start small. First, try participating in class when you're working with a small group, or participate only in your best subjects. Once you start to feel more comfortable, work your way up to situations that make you more nervous, like raising your hand at a school assembly or participating when you aren't 100% sure of the answer. It is also a good idea to use strategies that help you feel less nervous in the moment, like taking deep breaths or simply reminding yourself that you are brave and can do hard things.

Social anxiety is likely caused by your genetics and your environment. Your genetics are the traits that have been passed down to you from family members. So, if there are people in your family who have anxiety, you are more likely to have it too. Your environment, in this case, means the things you have experienced in your life. Because of both your genetics and your environment, your brain probably works in a slightly different way than the brains of people who do not have anxiety. Think of your brain like a smoke alarm—sometimes the alarm goes off because there is real danger and sometimes it is a false alarm. People with anxiety are more prone to false alarms and often have to learn ways to tell their body that it is a false alarm. Remember that anxiety is not your fault, and you should never feel bad about yourself just because your brain works in a slightly different way. You can work with a mental health professional to learn effective ways to prevent and cope with the false alarms of social anxiety, like breathing exercises, mantras, and other mindfulness techniques.

CHAPTER 2

MAKING CONNECTIONS

You've got the conversation basics down. Introducing yourself? No problem. But how do you really *connect* with others? Some girls make it look so easy. They're always together, whispering secrets and giggling, dropping little inside jokes that no one else understands. If you struggle to bond with others that way, you aren't alone.

The truth is, making connections usually takes time and patience. It helps if you know where to look for new friends who will share your interests and appreciate all the quirks and qualities that make you you. Once you find them, you'll want to find common ground—which means you have some things in common but you also respect one another's differences. Speaking of differences, you'll have an even better chance of connecting with others if you're mindful about being inclusive. Don't worry, we'll cover all of this and more in the pages ahead.

So, what's the secret to finding friends, both online and IRL? Do you just give someone a ton of compliments to make them like you? What about when you walk into a party and you don't know anyone? What if you want to try something new, but it means putting yourself out there in front of others? What if you have a crush, and all your conversation skills fly right out the window?

It's time to dive a little deeper. Let's go through the building blocks of connecting with others and building meaningful relationships.

WHERE ARE YOUR FUTURE FRIENDS?

Some kids go to a giant public school, others go to a smaller private school. They might live in a small town or a busy suburb or a big city. They might be homeschooled, or they might attend boarding school far away from home. Some are enrolled in virtual school full-time. But regardless of where they're from and what kinds of schools they attend, lots of kids have one thing in common: they have a hard time finding new friends.

You might be surrounded by thousands of kids at school every day. But maybe you don't feel like you have much in common with them, or your social anxiety is keeping you from really trying to connect. Here's the thing: your future friends probably share a few common interests with you. So the best way to start looking is to consider your passions and look for groups both inside and outside of school. Here are a few ideas:

* **Sports.** Maybe you're into team sports, like softball or basketball. Or individual sports, like martial arts or tennis, might be more your style. If your school doesn't offer the activity, check your community's parks and recreation website to find local leagues and camps.

* **Arts.** Band, choir, drama, and art classes are likely offered at your school. But don't forget to check local museums, theaters, and music schools for even more options.

* **Tech.** If your school doesn't have a coding or computer club, a nearby

> **WHAT THE REBELS SAY**
>
> "I met my best friend through our school's math class. We both helped each other through the parts we didn't understand."
> –Stella, 12, Florida, USA

community college might offer one for kids and teens. And there are lots of options online too—which means you could make a few new virtual friends.

* **Gaming.** Speaking of virtual friends, you're bound to find plenty fighting aliens or building empires in your favorite MMO (massively multiplayer online game).

* **Books.** Sure, you've already got lots of great fictional friends. But you might just meet a few readers who are as obsessed with the latest installment of your favorite fantasy series if you attend book clubs and other events at your local library and bookstores.

* **Environment.** If you're passionate about fighting climate change, you're not alone! Organizations like Green Kids Now offer lots of

opportunities for you to get involved. You might even start a local cleanup club yourself to meet like-minded kids—and it's a win for the planet too.

✳ **Volunteering.** Food pantries, animal shelters, tutoring—helping others doesn't just make you feel good, it's also a great way to branch out and meet lots of new potential friends.

Regardless of where and how you look for new friends, remember to be patient. It takes a lot more than one meetup to really bond with someone. Relax and allow the friendship to develop slowly—and don't forget to have fun!

20 Conversation Starters

Looking for some questions to ask to get to know new friends better? Try these!

1. Do you have any pets?
2. What's your favorite band or musician?
3. If you could eat only one meal for dinner for the rest of your life, what would it be?
4. What's the best birthday you've ever had?
5. Which superpower would you most like to have?
6. If you could time-travel, when and where would you go?
7. If you could meet one celebrity in person, who would you choose?
8. Would you rather travel into space or explore the ocean?
9. What's your favorite book?
10. Would you rather write a book, act in a TV show, create a video game, or have your own YouTube channel?
11. Do you want to be famous when you grow up?

12. If you were invisible for a day, what would you do?

13. If you could turn into any animal, which animal would you want to be?

14. If you could be an amazing dancer or an amazing singer, which one would you pick?

15. If you could change one thing about school, what would it be?

16. Do you know any jokes?

17. If you could travel anywhere, where would you go?

18. What's the weirdest dream you've ever had?

19. What would you do if you won the lottery?

20. What was the best day of your life?

How to Find Common Ground

Think about your closest friends. You probably have a lot in common with them, right? Maybe you all love the same sports teams, video games, or books. But what do you not have in common? Do you have different taste when it comes to fashion? Food? Movies? You might even have a friend who seems like your total opposite in every way—but you get along great anyway.

Then again, sometimes having opposing views can lead to conflict. If that's the case with you and a friend, what should you do next? You might be able to find common ground, which starts with understanding your worldview.

You might be thinking, "What's my worldview?"

WHAT THE REBELS SAY

"Never be afraid to be a poppy in a field of daffodils."
—Michaela DePrince, ballerina

Well, you already know everyone is unique—including you. Every experience in your life so far has shaped your worldview, or your beliefs about the world. It's like your own personal philosophy! What are your thoughts on bullying? Animal rights? Freedom of speech? All of that (and more!) makes up your worldview.

A person's worldview is usually a mix of facts and opinions. For example, let's say you live near a park that doesn't have doggie-bag stations. As a result, people aren't picking up after their dogs. The lack of doggie-bag stations is a fact. How you feel about it—and what you think should be done to address the issue—is your opinion.

But maybe you have a friend with a different opinion. You think the town should install doggie-bag stations. Your friend thinks dog owners should carry bags with them. Now you feel uncomfortable talking about the park with your friend. What's going on?

First of all, it's completely normal to have feelings of discomfort when you're experiencing conflict. And the more passionately you and your friend feel about the issue, the bigger the conflict will feel. But that doesn't mean you can't both find common ground. Just follow these steps:

* **Take a deep breath and relax.** It's awesome to be passionate, but it's easy to get defensive when someone disagrees with you.

* **Open your mind.** Remember, everyone is allowed to have opinions, just like you! If you want others to listen to your point of view, then you'll want to give them the same courtesy.

* **Practice active listening.** Sometimes, when someone else is talking, our brains race ahead and plan out everything we're going to say next. Do your best to focus on what your friend is saying so you truly understand where she's coming from—even if you don't agree.

* **Respond calmly and respectfully.** Without us realizing it, our tone can slip into being sarcastic, aggressive, or even straight-up mean. If you really want your point of view to be heard, make sure your delivery doesn't detract from your message.

* **Look for areas of agreement.** Sure, you and your friend have different opinions. But what do you agree on? Identifying those things can help ease the conflict and lead to a more productive chat.

Take the example of the park. You want your town to do something, while your friend thinks dog owners should be more responsible. What's the common ground here? There's a lot! You both care about making the park a clean place for everyone to enjoy. You both agree the lack of doggie bags is a problem. And you both want to find a solution.

Of course, you won't always be able to find common ground with everyone. Some people might have beliefs that are the exact opposite of yours. Never feel like you have to sacrifice or hide your own values to make someone else happy. Rebel Girls stand up for what they believe in.

HOW TO BE INCLUSIVE

Imagine walking into a crowded school cafeteria. You scan the faces, but none of your friends have lunch this period. Nervously, you approach a table of girls and point to an empty chair.

"Can I sit here?"

The girls look at one another. Then one replies, "Sorry, it's taken."

You hurry away, head hanging in embarrassment.

Being excluded pretty much never feels good. Sometimes, we might exclude someone without even meaning to. That's why it's important to be inclusive.

What does inclusion mean?

Well, it's the opposite of exclusion! Exclusive means that something is restricted or limited. Inclusive means everything (and everyone!) is included. When it comes to making connections and forming new friendships, inclusive

WHAT THE REBELS SAY

"When I was in school, there was a girl sitting by herself. I asked her to sit with me and my friends."
—Olivia, 9, New York, USA

34

is the way to go. After all, who wants to limit how many friends they can have? Meeting more people gives you more opportunities to learn and have fun.

Here are a few ways you can practice being inclusive:

✳ **Be curious about (and respectful of) other cultures.**

Sometimes, we might have an oversimplified idea of who a person is based on their culture—in other words, a stereotype. The best way to uncover and challenge any stereotypes you might have is to learn more about cultures outside of your own. For example, if you are white, you might read books that feature diverse characters and are written by BIPOC (Black, Indigenous, and people of color) authors. Whatever your background or heritage, you can watch shows or movies that feature experiences different from your own, or listen to music by artists from other cultures.

✳ **Step out of your comfort zone.** It's normal to feel comfortable around friends who are a lot like you. But it's also easy to slip into exclusive behavior without even realizing it. Remember, friendship isn't based on . . .

- Skin color
- Ability
- Gender
- Sexual orientation
- Religion
- Socio-economic status

You can be friends with anyone! Look for opportunities to connect with kids who seem a lot different from you on the surface—you'll be surprised at how much you have in common.

* **Challenge exclusion.** It's easy to think that exclusive behavior is harmless. But the truth is, it's a form of bullying. For example, deliberately inviting all but one classmate to an event in an attempt to hurt their feelings? That's exclusion—and it's bullying. If you notice others participating in this kind of behavior, challenge it! You might call them out on it. But if that sounds too scary, another option is to reach out to the excluded classmate and offer support and friendship.

* **Practice compassion.** The tricky thing about exclusion is that kids who practice it often feel like they're bonding with one another. For example, that group of girls who didn't allow you to sit in the empty chair at their cafeteria table? Excluding you might have made them feel like their friend group was special in some way. If you find yourself in a group like that, take a moment to put yourself in the shoes of the person being excluded. You know it feels terrible! Don't be afraid to reach out and show kindness to others, even if your friends aren't.

* **Celebrate individuality.** A kid who seems "different" in some way might be excluded and bullied. But remember, it's awesome that we're all so unique. It's our different quirks and qualities that make us all special. Finally, remember that being inclusive doesn't mean you have to tolerate cruelty or negative treatment. It also doesn't mean you have to be friends with literally everyone. Keep an open mind about your friends—the new and the old. And if you simply don't get along with someone, that's totally fine. There's a difference between exclusion and just keeping a respectful distance.

WHAT THE REBELS SAY

"It's okay to be quirky, it's fine to be shy. You don't have to go with the crowd."
—Alek Wek, supermodel

HOW TO GIVE AND RECEIVE COMPLIMENTS

Giving someone a compliment is a surefire way to brighten their day. It's also a great way to break the ice when you meet someone new. But giving a compliment isn't always as easy as it sounds. What exactly should you compliment? Do you really mean it, or does it sound insincere? How much is too much when it comes to compliments?

Hey, you've got this! After all, you're a smart, confident, kind Rebel Girl. (See how easy that was?) Here are some helpful do's and don'ts when it comes to giving compliments:

* **Do get specific!** Adding details to your compliment shows the recipient that you've truly noticed their greatness. For example, instead of "You're a great cook," you might say, "Your snickerdoodle cookies are my favorite because you use extra cinnamon."

* **Don't say it if you don't mean it.** Ever heard someone say something and thought to yourself, "You don't really mean that?" Most of us have a pretty good radar when it comes to what's sincere and what isn't. If you want to compliment someone, great! But if you can't come up with genuine praise in the moment, it's better not to say anything at all.

* **Do follow up with a question.** Receiving compliments can feel awkward sometimes (more on that soon). To help make the recipient feel more comfortable—and more flattered—come up with a question to ask after your compliment. For example, "I love that skirt! Where did you get it?" or "You have an amazing voice! What singer is your biggest inspiration?"

✳ **Don't focus on physical appearance.** Telling someone they're attractive is well-intentioned. But lots of kids are self-conscious about how they look—and you want your compliment to make them feel good, not anxious. If you want to compliment someone's appearance, make sure it's something they have control over, like their sense of style and fashion. For example, instead of "You have pretty hair," you might say, "I love your haircut!"

✳ **Do focus on achievements.** When we achieve something amazing, it's a great feeling—and it's nice when someone notices. If you want to compliment someone, ask yourself what they're probably most proud of right now: an awesome math test score? A recent game-winning soccer goal? Praise away!

* **Don't go overboard.** It's easy to offer too much of a good thing. Complimenting someone too much or too frequently might make them uncomfortable—or even cause them to wonder if you're looking for praise in return.

Now let's take a look at the flip side. How do you feel when someone compliments you? Maybe you can't get enough . . . or maybe it makes you squirm a little bit. You might even feel kind of bad. Thoughts like, "That's not true" or "I don't deserve that" might spring up in your mind. Before you know it, you're putting yourself down or deflecting the compliment—even if you truly deserve it!

Accepting a compliment can make us feel like we're walking a tightrope. If we lean too far one way and act like we totally deserve the praise, we might fall into arrogance. But if we lean too far the other way and reject the compliment, we risk becoming self-deprecating (in other words, making yourself or what you do seem unimportant).

So how can you accept a compliment without tumbling off the rope? Follow these simple steps:

* **Say thank you.** Yes, it's really that easy! Even if you feel you don't deserve the praise, show your appreciation to the person who offered it.
* **Explain why you appreciate the compliment.** For example, let's say you just took your first ballet class. You felt super out of step the whole time, but a kind girl compliments you on your plié. Instead of brushing her off or talking about how terrible you thought you were, you could say, "Thanks! I felt kind of awkward, but that makes me want to practice even more."
* **Acknowledge others if appropriate.** You just crossed the finish line first during a relay at a track meet. Your coach and teammates are no doubt lavishing you with well-earned praise—acknowledging their efforts

and achievements in return will help you feel less awkward about the compliments. (Plus, your teammates deserve it too!)

* **Only reciprocate if you mean it.** Remember how we talked about sensing insincerity? Sometimes, complimenting someone in return happens almost as an instinct. But if you don't really mean it, don't say it. When someone compliments you, it's completely fine to say, "Thanks, I appreciate that," and move on.

HOW TO TRY SOMETHING NEW

Maybe it's joining a community theater group, or trying out for the track team, or signing up for coding club—whatever it is, you're *obsessed*. You imagine yourself standing onstage to wild applause, or crossing that finish line, or coding an incredible game, and goosebumps break out all over your arms.

Then you picture yourself flubbing your lines, or coming in last place, or never getting the hang of coding, and your skin crawls.

Nope. You're way too scared to try.

Failure is super scary. It can make us feel defeated, disappointed, and embarrassed. But failure is nothing to be ashamed of. In fact, failure is the key to success!

Think about all the things you're great at now, like riding a bike or swimming or doing a cartwheel. Did you do all those things perfectly the first time? Probably not. Maybe you started with training wheels on your bike, and you had a few falls when you took them off. Maybe you started out wearing a life jacket, and getting in the pool without one for the first time made you anxious. Maybe your first cartwheel ended with you landing flat on your butt!

WHAT THE REBELS SAY

"When you're trying something new, remember to breathe and focus."
—Raffy L., 14, Connecticut, USA

Those experiences might have been scary (or even a little bit funny). But the point is, you learned from them, and you tried again and again until you nailed it. Failure isn't permanent. It's actually the opposite! Failure is a chance to learn how to get *better*.

Reframe Failure

When you are considering trying something new, grab a journal or a piece of paper and answer the following prompts.

* *Best-case scenario.* Write down all the reasons this new thing excites you and all the wonderful things that might happen if you try. Dream BIG—the sky's the limit!

* *Worst-case scenario.* Write down all your worst fears of what might go wrong if you try. Add as many details as possible—even if it gets silly. (Sometimes, our fears are kind of funny.)

* *Turn it around!* Write down what you can do if each one of those fears comes true. How exactly would you react? What could you learn from this? How could you improve? And most importantly, why would this be *empowering*, not embarrassing?

You might not like every new thing you try . . . but you won't know until you give it a shot.

WHAT TO DO WHEN YOU WALK INTO A PARTY AND DON'T KNOW ANYONE

So you're ready to make new friends, to try new things with confidence, to be brave—and you accept an invitation to a party. Awesome!

But when you walk in the room and look around for a familiar face or two, you don't see any.

Like, at all.

Gulp. You don't know anyone here. Now what?

Never fear! Here are a few tips to help you have a blast (and maybe even make a few new friends):

* **Offer to help the host.** Hosting a party is fun, but it's also a lot of work. Look for whoever's throwing the party (even if you've never met her before) and ask if she needs help with anything. It'll show your appreciation for being invited, not to mention give you something to do.

* **Try on an extroverted personality.** Hey, if you don't know anyone here, that means they don't know you! Now's the perfect time to see what it feels like to be an extrovert without any friends giving you the side-eye or asking, "Why are you acting so different?"

* **Ask questions.** Remember, questions help keep the conversation going. Even something as simple as "What song is this?" can get a group chatting for hours.

* **Pocket your phone.** When you don't know anyone in the room, it's tempting to see what everyone's up to on TikTok. But staring at your screen will discourage others from approaching you.

* **Look for lone wolves.** Chances are, you aren't the only person here who doesn't know anyone. See that girl over there in the corner? Go say hi!

* **Bring snacks.** This one takes a little pre-party preparation, but it's worth it. Delicious treats are a great icebreaker. Plus, if you made them yourself, you can tell people the recipe.

Picture This

Andrea is super excited about her first day at a new school—but she's also nervous. She really wants to make friends. On her first day, her guidance counselor recommends that she try a few different extracurricular activities.

It's definitely a great way to meet kids with similar interests. But Andrea has always been pretty shy. She hangs out on the bleachers and watches the basketball team practice. The girls all seem nice, but she isn't really into sports.

Next, she sits in on choir rehearsal. Andrea loves belting out Taylor Swift songs alone in her room, but singing in a group just isn't her thing.

Andrea tries a ton of clubs during her first week: photography, drama, gaming, gardening, origami, robotics. The kids in all of these clubs are friendly . . . but Andrea doesn't feel like she's clicking with them. Mostly because she can't seem to find an activity she's passionate about, like all the other kids seem to be.

Just as she's about to give up, she sees a girl named Jasmine handing out flyers in the cafeteria. The local animal shelter desperately needs volunteers after school and on the weekends.

"Do you like animals?" Jasmine asks.

Andrea laughs. "I have a dog, two cats, and three guinea pigs at home."

"Wow!" Jasmine exclaims. "I think you'd love volunteering at the animal shelter. I hope you come."

That afternoon, Andrea arrives at the animal shelter. She's just as nervous as she was trying out all the other activities—but this time, she's excited too. She looks around eagerly at all of the dogs and cats.

When she sees Jasmine standing with a group of kids, Andrea's stomach flutters. Now she has to introduce herself and figure out what to talk about. It's so intimidating! When Jasmine looks up, Andrea smiles and waves. Jasmine beams and gestures for Andrea to join them.

"Guys, this is Andrea, our newest volunteer," she says. "She has so many pets at home."

"Awesome!" says another girl. "Do you have any pictures?"

"Of course!" Andrea pulls out her phone as the others gather around. Soon, they're all talking and giggling, sharing stories about their pets. Andrea is thrilled. It turns out that making friends was easier than she thought.

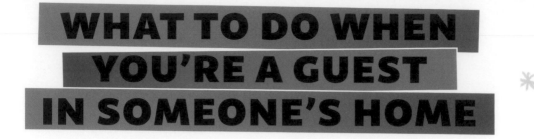

WHAT TO DO WHEN YOU'RE A GUEST IN SOMEONE'S HOME

The first time you visit a friend's home can be a little intimidating—and it might even cause anxiety. Things are bound to be different from life in your house! For example, your family might have a rule that everyone leaves their shoes at the front door so no one tracks mud in the house. But kicking off your shoes upon stepping inside a friend's home might cause confusion with your hosts.

In general, you should follow the rules of the house. If you don't know all of those rules, that's totally okay—don't be afraid to ask your friend to explain them. Here are some solid ground rules that apply pretty much anytime you're a guest:

* **Be polite.** When we're with our friends, we might goof around a lot—and our manners might go out the window. But when you're around your friend's family, acting silly can come off as disrespectful. Don't forget to greet other family members who might be home and thank them for the invitation.

* **Use table manners.** That means washing your hands before you eat, chewing with your mouth closed, and putting your napkin in your lap. Of course, you should follow your friend's lead here! If she has permission to bring popcorn up to her room so you two can watch your favorite show together, it's fine to go along with her.

* **Clean up after yourself.** Whether it's offering to help with the dishes after dinner or wiping up that bit of nail polish you accidentally smeared on the bathroom counter, show respect for your friend's family and their home by keeping it clean.

Special Sleepover Rules

What's more fun than a sleepover with your besties? Pretty much nothing! If it's your first time spending the night at a friend's house, keep the following tips in mind.

* Bring your own toiletries.
* Ask permission before using any computers or tablets in the house.
* Avoid snooping around in cabinets and closets!
* Keep the volume down, especially when it gets late.
* Offer to help your friend clean up before you leave in the morning.

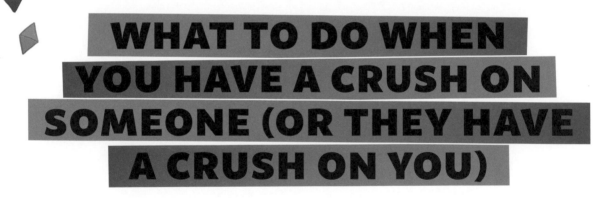

WHAT TO DO WHEN YOU HAVE A CRUSH ON SOMEONE (OR THEY HAVE A CRUSH ON YOU)

You probably know that having a crush on someone means you like them. Maybe you've seen how your friend acts around her crush and you think to yourself, "Wow, her feelings are super obvious!"

But when it's happening to you, it's not always so obvious—or easy!

Maybe you just met someone. Or maybe you've known them for a long time. But suddenly, you find yourself thinking about them. Like, a *lot*. You feel strange when they're around—kind of nervous, but also kind of giddy. You find yourself copying some of their mannerisms. You never realized how awesome their favorite band is until now. And that video game they're into that never really interested you? Now, you're *super* into it.

Having a crush on someone can be really exciting, but also a little scary. Do you tell them how you feel? What if they don't feel the same way? What if they *do*—now what?!

First of all, don't be embarrassed or ashamed. You don't have to tell everyone about your crush, but you don't have to keep it a secret, either. Your crush might only last a few days, or it might build over months. There's no rule on when you have to share— or who you have to share it with.

Next, find a way to explore your feelings privately—journaling is a great option here! Be honest with yourself about your crush. How well do you know them? Are they a close friend, and suddenly your feelings have changed? Why? Or is this someone you've been admiring from afar? Sometimes, we create a fantasy version of others in our minds, especially when it comes to celebrities and influencers. But this can also happen with people we know IRL. This is normal, but it's important to recognize when your crush might be on your *idea* of someone, rather than who they really are.

Last but not least, enjoy the feeling while it lasts. Studies show that having a crush on someone increases your serotonin levels. Serotonin is a hormone that helps you feel happy. That's right—having a crush is scientifically proven to make you more positive, so embrace it!

How Do I Tell My Crush How I Feel?

If you've been crushing on someone for a while, you might feel like you want to tell them and see if the feelings are mutual. That's exciting! But it can be scary. Here are some tips for putting yourself out there in that way:

* *Talk to your crush.* Ask questions that will help you get to know them better before you spill all your feelings.

* *Tell them privately.* Telling someone you *like them* like them while you're surrounded by friends can make an already awkward moment even more awkward. Not just for you, but for your crush too. Regardless of how they feel about you, the reactions of your peers (especially if there's teasing involved) will affect how they respond to your confession. So find a time and a place where there aren't too many other people around, like when you're walking home from school together.

* *Keep it short and sweet.* "You're really nice, and I like you as more than a friend. I wondered if you might feel the same way." It might be tempting to gush about all the reasons you find your crush wonderful, but doing so might make them feel uncomfortable.

* *Be prepared for the best—and the worst.* If your crush reciprocates your feelings, that's amazing! But if they want to remain friends, it's important to be respectful of that.

* *Remember, you don't have to tell your crush if you don't want to.* Just because you like someone doesn't mean you're obligated to let them know, or even date them. You might just want to enjoy the feeling and keep it all to yourself.

How Do I Get Over a Crush?

Getting over a crush can feel absolutely impossible. The pain is *real*, and we're positive we'll never feel this way about anyone else, ever. But as hard as it might be to believe, you will recover!

* **Have patience.** Getting over a crush is a process—sometimes, a very *long* process. Don't try and push away your sadness and disappointment. Those are normal feelings, so let yourself feel them.

* **Process your emotions.** Maybe it's a bubble bath with a fantasy novel. Maybe it's jumping on a trampoline and singing along to your favorite playlist at the top of your lungs. Find a fun way to soothe—or release—those negative emotions.

* **Find a confidant.** It might be your best friend, your grown-up, a sibling—anyone you trust to listen and sympathize with what you're going through. Talking about our negative feelings pretty much always helps them feel a little less negative.

* **Try not to obsess.** It can be tempting to fixate on your crush even more, especially on social media. But that's only going to make you feel worse. Instead, distract yourself with new hobbies, find fun new accounts to follow online, and focus on you, not your crush.

What If Someone Has a Crush on Me?!

It starts with a smile in the hall on the way to your locker. Then a comment and a heart on your latest Insta photo. Soon you're wondering, *Are they just being nice, or do they* like *me?*

Being crushed on can cause all kinds of feelings! You're probably flattered. It might make you feel excited, or nervous, or a mix of both.

So how do you handle it? First off, remind yourself what it feels like when you have a crush on someone. If this person does have those feelings for you, they're in a pretty vulnerable place. However you handle it, make sure you treat them kindly and with respect.

Should I just ask them if they like me? Maybe. It depends on the person and how well you know them. Asking such a direct question can make someone feel exposed or even embarrassed, and that's the last thing you want. If this is someone you don't know all that well, try getting to know them a little better first. (They could just be the kind of person who smiles at everyone.) If this is a really good friend, it's okay to ask—but remember to keep it kind, not accusatory.

I think I might like them too, but I'm not sure. Now what? Here's the good news: there's no need to rush! Take your time and allow yourself to explore your feelings (again, journaling can help here). Try hanging out with your maybe-crush in a group setting a few times so you can spend time with them without leading them on or making them think it's a date.

I'm not interested in them "that way." How can I let them down gently? Try this: wait until a moment when the two of you are alone. If they haven't outright told you they have a crush on you, tell them how much you value their friendship. If they've confessed their feelings, tell them you're really flattered but you'd prefer to remain good friends. This conversation can feel extra awkward, but you'll both feel so much better in the long run.

I don't want to date them . . . but I kind of like the attention. Of course you do! Everyone likes to be liked. But remember, another person's feelings are on the line here. The last thing you want to do is lead them on and make them think you *do* want to date them, only to break their heart later. There's absolutely nothing wrong with flirting, but if you think the other person has a crush on you and you don't feel the same way, the kind thing to do is treat them like a friend and nothing more.

I don't want to date them, and I really DON'T like the attention. They told you they like you. You told them you just want to be friends. But they're still flirting and giving you unwanted attention. That's not okay! It's time to find a trusted adult and let them know this person is making you feel uncomfortable.

HOW TO MAKE FRIENDS SAFELY ONLINE

Internet might as well mean "infinite" because that's how many potential friends there are online. That's exciting, but also kind of overwhelming. Where should you start looking? How do you know the kids you meet are really who they say they are? Can you really form as close a bond with someone online as you can IRL? Here are a few tips to remember when you hop online looking for friendship:

* **Be choosy with your apps.** There are tons of apps out there kids use to meet up and chat. Before you download one, take a few minutes to research the app itself. Does it have a few verification measures that make

users prove they are who they say they are? If it's pretty easy to get on there anonymously, it's probably not the best place to look for friends.

* **Take care not to overshare.** Setting up a new profile can be fun! We want to showcase our awesome personalities. But make sure you don't share too many specific details, especially when it comes to things like where you live and go to school. Depending on the app, you can customize your privacy settings to limit who can view your posts.

* **Check your selfie backgrounds.**
There's nothing wrong with sharing your beaming face with your new online friends. Before you post, double-check the background to make sure you aren't broadcasting your location . . . or a pile of dirty laundry.

* **Share with IRL friends and family.** Having secrets can be fun sometimes. But it's not a good idea to keep an online friendship or a new chat app a secret. If you're hitting it off with friends online, that's great! Just tell a few trusted friends or family members about it.

* **Trust your gut.** Curiosity is totally normal. But if you find yourself talking to someone online or exploring a new forum or chat feature on a game that feels *off* in any way, that's your instinct kicking in—and you should honor that feeling. Don't be afraid to block anyone who's giving you unwanted attention, and make sure to tell a trusted adult what's going on.

Where Should You Look for a New Friend?

1. **This weekend, you get to do literally anything you want. What's it going to be?**

   A. Playing along with my favorite gamer's livestream.
   B. I saw a cool tutorial for DIY earrings made out of feathers. I might give that a try!
   C. Two words: ROLLER. DERBY.
   D. There's a march to raise awareness of climate change, and that's the only place I want to be.

2. **Your principal announces that students will get to vote on a brand-new club at your school. Which one is your top choice?**

   A. Astronomy Club. Using giant telescopes to see the planets and stars? Yes, please!
   B. Improv Club. Making up scenes and stories on the spot? Nothing could be more fun than that.
   C. Zombie Survival Club. We'd learn basic survival tactics and some martial arts. Plus lots of running!
   D. Cultural Exchange Club. Festivals, food, music, even international movie nights—sounds like a fun way to learn and appreciate other cultures.

3. **Your family goes on a mega-awesome vacation to a resort, and you're looking at the list of available activities. Which one are you most excited to try?**

   A. There's a massive arcade, and I'm basically going to live there.
   B. A sandcastle competition. Mine's going to be EPIC.
   C. Definitely kayaking! Or parasailing! Or snorkeling! Hang on: zip-lining!
   D. The nature walk with a local tour guide. I'm so curious about the local wildlife.

4. **Your friends are trying to pick a movie to watch at a sleepover party. Which one gets your vote?**

   A. A sci-fi movie, or maybe a historical one . . . something that's gonna make me think.
   B. Which one looks the wackiest?

I love a movie that's "out there."

C. Action, thriller, superhero flick—anything that gets my blood pumping!

D. A good documentary, or a biopic about someone who changed the world for the better.

5. **Your teacher assigns a book report, and you get to choose any book you want. What kind of book do you tell the librarian you're looking for?**

A. Got anything notoriously difficult to read? I'm up for the challenge.

B. I want a book that defies genre— or maybe mixes all the genres together.

C. I'd love to find a memoir by an Olympic medalist.

D. I prefer nonfiction . . . or maybe a translated novel published in another country.

6. **If you had to pick your future career right now, which one of these is the closest fit?**

A. Astronaut

B. Actress

C. Athlete

D. Ambassador

7. **Snow day! School is officially closed and you're completely free. What's the plan?**

A. I've got a 5,000-piece puzzle, and I'm about to set a record.

B. Put on my favorite playlist and pull out the arts and crafts supplies.

C. No time to talk—I'm looking for my sled . . .

D. Bake tons of treats to share with everyone at school tomorrow.

Mostly As: The Geeky Group

Your brain loves a good challenge! Why not surround yourself with like-minded folks? Clubs that focus on robotics, coding, chess, books, debate, and gaming are great places for you to make new friends. If your school or local community doesn't offer the activities you're interested in, ask a parent or teacher to help you find a group online.

Mostly Bs: The Creative Crew

Whether it's painting, writing, or making music, you love to express yourself creatively. Art, choir, band, orchestra, photography, dance, and theater clubs are no doubt filled with future friends waiting for you. If none of those really suits you, don't be afraid to think outside the box. Maybe you want to learn how to make puppets, or create your own jewelry, or get into graphic design. Why not start your own club and let creative friends find you?

Mostly Cs: The Active Assembly

There's no doubt about it—you love to move! Maybe it's through team sports like volleyball, track, basketball, or softball. Or perhaps you prefer ballet, tap, or contemporary dance. How about gardening, hiking, biking, skateboarding, swimming, yoga, martial arts, horseback riding? The possibilities are endless, and there's sure to be a group out there just for kids like you who put the *active* in activities.

Mostly Ds: The Community Club

Hobbies are great, but hobbies that help others are the ones for you! Volunteering at places like animal shelters, food pantries, environmental groups, and cleanup crews can be fun, fulfilling, and a great way to make new friends. At school, consider student council, the yearbook staff, the newspaper staff, and tutoring—all fun activities that allow you to meet more kids while contributing to the whole student body.

ASK THE EXPERT

Cara Goodwin, PhD
Child Psychologist

How can you make it easier on yourself
when you try new things?
—Zooey, 11, Kentucky, USA

Trying new things is difficult for all of us, but there are definitely ways to make it easier. First, try to learn as much as possible about the thing you are about to try. Do your research and ask people questions to make the new thing feel as familiar as possible. Then ease into it gradually. For example, if you're joining a soccer team for the first time, kick the ball around your yard or local park with a friend or sibling before your first practice. Finally, remember the more frequently you try new things, the easier it will get!

How do you make new friends when you move a lot?
—Naomi, 8, New Mexico, USA

I also moved a lot as a kid, so I know how hard it can be! My advice would be to join new clubs, sports, and groups right away—sharing interests with other kids is the fastest way to make friends. When you go to new places or events, put away your phone or any other distractions, and try to look for people your age to introduce yourself to. You could also host a get-together for your new classmates or neighbors. Lastly, remember to smile and introduce yourself to all the new kids you meet at school, sports practices, or clubs—you never know who will end up being your good friend.

CHAPTER 3

COMMUNICATION IS KEY

Okay, you've got the basics down: how to introduce yourself, how to find new friends, how to handle situations that might cause social anxiety. You're trying new things with confidence, and you're making connections and forming great relationships.

You're starting to realize how important communication is—even when it feels super awkward. Like when someone asks you for a favor, and even though you want to make them happy, you have to say no. Or when you find yourself struggling at school and you need to talk to your teacher about it. Or when someone you love is intruding on your personal space, and you aren't sure how to tell them without hurting their feelings.

When we have social anxiety, it often feels like the solution is just to make everyone else happy all the time. Because if they're all happy, there's nothing to feel anxious about! But when we constantly put our friends and family members' needs and wants above our own, it makes our own anxiety worse in the long run.

That's why this chapter is all about creating and maintaining a healthy social life. That means learning about boundaries, asking for help, and speaking up for yourself—whether you're an introvert, an extrovert, or anywhere in between.

HOW TO SAY NO

No is another two-letter word that, like *hi*, should be easy to say . . . but sometimes, it's just not. Like when a kid in your math class offers to show you the test answers she swiped from the teacher's desk. Or when a friend's sister offers to drive you both to the mall, but you know she doesn't have a driver's license yet. You know it's a bad idea. You don't want to do it.

So why is it so hard to say no?

Well, lots of reasons! You don't want to hurt someone's feelings. You don't want to make someone mad or disappoint them. You don't want to get teased or laughed at. Just the thought of it makes you anxious! And in that moment, saying yes makes that anxiety go away—but only temporarily.

Peer pressure happens every day. And it's not always a bad thing. Your peers—basically, your friends and any other kids around you at school and elsewhere—can encourage you to try new things and help you develop important social skills. But peer pressure can also lead to doing things that make you uncomfortable and even risk getting you into trouble.

In those moments, you probably feel torn. On the one hand, you don't want to do what your peers are pressuring you to do. On the other hand, how are they going to react if you say no? *What if they make fun of me? What if they hate me?* All those "what ifs" are enough to make our brains turn a no into an "okay, I guess."

But you really want to say no. And all those "what ifs?" They might not even happen! The kid with the math test answers might tease . . . or she might just

62

shrug and say okay. Your friend might be disappointed when you turn down her sister's offer to drive you both to the mall . . . or she might look relieved and admit she was nervous about going too.

Here are a few different ways you can say no, depending on the situation:

* **I'd rather not, because . . .** Offer a specific reason why you're declining, such as what might happen if you get caught. It's possible your peers hadn't considered your reasons, and they could change their minds.

* **I have an idea! Instead, why don't we . . .** Suggest an alternative activity—one that you feel comfortable with and that you think everyone else will enjoy too.

* **That sounds fun, but I can't because . . .** Make up an excuse. Yes, even if it's not true. In some cases, it's totally fine to tell a little white lie to get out of a potentially uncomfortable situation.

* **Sorry, I have to go.** Excuse yourself and walk away. If you can't bring yourself to say no but you really don't want to say yes, just leave!
* **Nah, I'm good.** Smile, shrug, and shake your head. Your peers might ask why, but you don't have to offer an explanation.

How to Set and Respect Boundaries

You know how characters in video games often have a little symbol that indicates how much energy they have left? As they move through the game, their energy slowly drains until they're running on empty.

Talk about relatable.

How many times have you felt awesome first thing in the morning, but with every hour that passes—hours filled with stressful situations like telling your best friend you can't come to her soccer match, getting called on in class when you don't know the answer, dealing with having a massive crush on your lab partner, and like a million other moments of anxiety—you can practically see your little energy symbol draining until you've got nothing left?

It happens to all of us! That's where boundaries come in. Whether you realize it or not, you probably already have a few boundaries in place that everyone in your life knows about. Does your family know not to disturb you before ten o'clock on Saturday mornings because you like to sleep in? Do your friends know you can't hang out after school on Tuesdays because that's when you go to the library? Those are examples of boundaries that you put in place at some point.

So, how do you set boundaries? Start by answering the following questions (the more specific, the better!):

* What makes me feel energized?
* What drains my energy?
* What part of the day am I looking forward to the most?
* What part of the day am I looking forward to the least?
* What makes me feel safe?
* What makes me feel unsafe?
* What makes me feel valued?
* What makes me feel taken advantage of?
* What relaxes me the most?
* What stresses me out the most?

It's important to remember that setting boundaries isn't an excuse for avoiding necessary things. For example, most of us don't look forward to going to the dentist. But deciding to never go to the dentist again isn't setting a boundary—it's bad oral hygiene! Instead, remind yourself that having clean, healthy teeth is something you look forward to.

Let's say one thing that makes you feel taken advantage of is your sister constantly borrowing your clothes without asking. This is your chance to set a boundary with her.

Set a boundary with someone using these three steps:

* ✷ **Consider their point of view first.** Chances are, they aren't actually trying to stress you out or make you feel bad.

* ✷ **Avoid accusations.** Focus on your request—you don't have to point out how bad their actions made you feel.

* ✷ **Explain how this boundary will help you.** Offer a specific example if possible.

Here's how you might set a boundary with your sister about your clothes: Say to her, "Hey, can I ask you a favor? I love that we can share clothes, and that skirt you borrowed looks awesome on you. Would you mind asking me before you borrow my clothes next time? I like to plan my outfits for the week, and that would help me out a ton."

What Types of Boundaries Can I Set?

Any kind! A few examples:

✳ *Your energy.* "I had a pretty intense week. This weekend, I'm going to do a little self-care instead of going to the game."

✳ *Your emotions.* "I'm still sad about my guinea pig dying. Can I please stay inside during recess and write in my journal instead?"

✳ *Your chats.* "Talking about the hurricane is making me feel anxious. Can we change the subject?"

✳ *Your stuff.* "Yes, you can borrow my book—but please use a bookmark instead of folding down the pages."

✳ *Your socials.* "I'm a little uncomfortable with how I look in that video. Would you mind not posting it, or maybe editing me out?"

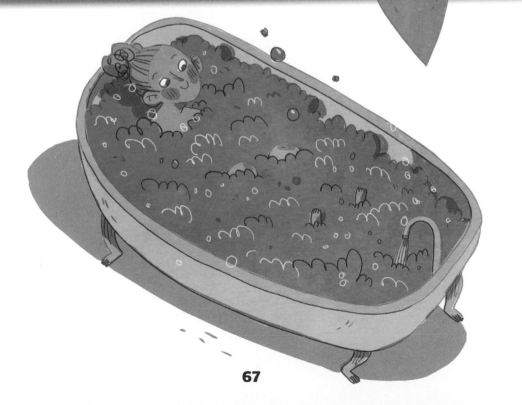

HOW TO ASK FOR HELP

Pop quiz! Asking for help is . . .

A. Annoying

B. A sign of weakness

C. An inconvenience

D. None of the above

The answer is *D. None of the above*, of course! But the first three feel real sometimes, don't they? When we know we need help and we think about asking someone, we have a lot of fears. Will they be annoyed? Will they think we're weak?

But when someone you care about asks you for help, is that what *you* think? Probably not! In fact, you might feel proud that they trust you enough to ask. Plus, it's nice to feel needed and valued.

Everyone needs help sometimes. And asking for help is a sign of maturity, not weakness. Whether you're struggling with a subject in school, a problem with a friend, instances of bullying, or mental health issues, asking for help is the best—and bravest—thing you can do.

To make it feel a little less awkward, keep the following tips in mind.

✳ **Choose carefully.**
   Who are you turning
   to for help with this
   particular issue—and

why? What are they going through right now? Make sure you take their current situation into consideration before approaching them. For example, if your best friend has recently learned her grandmother is ill, it might not be the best time to ask her for advice on an argument you had with your parents.

* **Speak openly.** The awkwardness we feel when asking for help can often lead to us beating around the bush. It's like we're hoping the other person will guess what we need without us having to ask. But unless your friends and family can read minds, that's an expectation that's bound to leave you disappointed. Consider rehearsing your request for help beforehand so you know exactly what you're going to say.

* **Remember that you aren't doing anything wrong.** Have you ever started your request for help with an apology? "I'm really sorry, but I was wondering if . . . " Hey, no one needs to apologize for needing help! And you don't have to offer something in return, either. Most people love to lend a helping hand when asked, no strings attached.

* **Share your results.** After someone helps you out, make sure to let them know how everything turned out. This—along with saying thank you, of course—demonstrates how much you appreciate their assistance.

Now, let's try another quiz. Asking for help is . . .

  A. Mature
  B. Brave

C. Sometimes scary—but I can do it!

D. All of the above

The answer is *D. All of the above*, of course!

How to Ask for a Favor

Wait, isn't asking for a favor basically asking for help? Yes . . . and no. When you do someone a favor, you're obviously helping them out. But in general, help is something we *need*, and favors are something we *want*. One is necessary, and the other makes our lives a little more convenient.

✳ When a friend loses her necklace on the bus and asks for you to search with her, she *needs* your help.

✳ When a friend asks if she can borrow your necklace, she *wants* a favor.

Asking for a favor isn't much different than asking for help. You definitely want to take the person you're asking into consideration. Is this a good time for them? Will granting this favor cost them anything (not just financially, but emotionally or in regards to their time)? Be clear that you're asking for a favor—dropping hints isn't the way to go here. It's better to be upfront and honest.

Finally, make it clear that there are no hard feelings if they have to refuse. And no matter how they respond, make sure to thank them for considering the favor in the first place.

WHAT THE REBELS SAY

"There can be times that are tougher than others. For me, reaching out to other folks really helped me get through those moments."
—America Ferrera, actor and activist

70

HOW TO DEAL WHEN YOU'RE STRUGGLING IN SCHOOL

Let's be real: school is stressful. Some days are great—you coast through your classes, ace your tests, and have a ton of fun with your friends. Other days, it feels like you can't do anything right. You forgot your homework at home. You didn't study for a quiz and totally bomb. Your teacher catches you spacing out during class and calls you out in front of everyone.

It's not just embarrassing. It's *frustrating*. And sometimes, there's kind of a snowball effect. One bad day is followed by another, then another, and suddenly it seems like your whole semester is a hot mess. You know it's time to talk to your teachers. But just thinking about it makes you feel overwhelmed. Where do you even begin to explain? Don't worry! We've got some tips.

* **Schedule a time.** If you spring the conversation on your teacher right after class, she might not be ready to really listen and discuss it with you. Simply stop by her desk and say, "Can we meet after school to talk about my grade?" Having a scheduled appointment will give you both time to prepare for the chat.

* **Make it one-on-one.** Chatting with your teacher before or after class, with lots of other kids coming in and out of the room, is only going

to stress you out even more. Before or after school or your teacher's conference period is your best bet for a quiet, private discussion.

* **Prep ahead of time.** Consider writing down exactly what you're going to say. You might even want to practice saying it out loud, particularly if you're extra anxious.

* **Be specific.** "I'm struggling" can mean lots of different things. Do you find your mind wandering during class? Is this particular unit especially difficult for you? Are you doing great in class but struggling with the homework? The more details you give your teacher, the better they'll be able to help you.

* **Share your anxiety.** Here's the thing about anxiety—everyone experiences it, including teachers! Whether you're feeling more anxious in class lately, or you've been diagnosed with general anxiety disorder, OCD, or anything else that is impacting how you learn, share as much as you're comfortable sharing with your teacher.

* **Tell them what they can do to help.** You might already have an idea of how your teacher can help ease your struggle. You might explain that getting called on in class causes you to freeze up and request that your teacher call on you only if you raise your hand. If your mind is wandering, you could ask to be moved to a desk closer to the front of the class.

HOW TO TAKE CRITICISM

Even the word *criticize* can make us flinch. Receiving negative feedback can sting a little. And if the criticism is harsh, it might sting a *lot*.

But the truth is that criticism isn't a bad thing—it's how we learn, grow, and improve. Think of anyone you admire: musicians, actors, influencers, writers, politicians, scientists. Every single one of them has experienced criticism—and lots of it.

Let's say you wrote a short story. It's the first time you've ever written fiction, and you're incredibly proud. The characters feel real, you created a really cool fantasy world, and there's even a shocking twist ending. Honestly? It's *awesome*.

You work up your courage and let a few friends or family members read it. They praise your brilliance, and you're basking in all the love. Maybe you'll even turn this thing into a novel! Then your best friend—who's read, like, every fantasy novel ever—points out a flaw in your story's magic system.

A *big* flaw.

It feels like a gut punch. You worked *so hard* on this. Is that flaw really a problem? No one else mentioned it. Why is your bestie being so mean?

The truth is, she's not being mean—she's offering honest, constructive criticism. And it's not meant to make you feel bad about your story. It's meant to help take your already great story and make it *even better*.

Here are a few tips on how to handle criticism:

* **Take a beat before you respond.** No matter how prepared you are for feedback, it can still sting. That's okay! It's like ripping off a bandage—it usually only hurts for a second.

* **Ask questions.** The more detailed and specific the feedback, the more helpful it will be for you. Plus, asking questions about the criticism can help lessen any anxiety you or your critic are feeling.

* **Decide your next step.** You're ready to improve. Now what? Coming up with an action plan will help you feel positive and motivated.

If you asked a friend for feedback and they offered constructive criticism, don't forget to thank them. Giving honest criticism can often cause just as much anxiety as accepting it. Make sure your friend knows she didn't hurt your feelings and that you value her opinion and support.

Picture This

Zoe is super into fashion, and she loves creating looks that express her personal sense of style. Her Aunt Rose is really supportive of this, and she enjoys giving Zoe clothes, shoes, and accessories as gifts.

The only problem is, Aunt Rose's taste is way different than Zoe's. Aunt Rose tends to choose soft fabrics in pastel colors. Zoe likes to experiment with bright colors and unusual combinations, like flannel shirts over lace dresses or overalls paired with a lime green blazer.

For Zoe's birthday, Aunt Rose sends her a very pretty yellow sweater . . . but it's just not her style. Zoe knows her aunt means well, and she really appreciates the gift. But she also feels guilty because she probably won't wear it.

"What should I do?" Zoe asks her mom. "I can't tell Aunt Rose I don't like it. That would hurt her feelings!"

"That's true," her mom says thoughtfully. "But I'm pretty sure Aunt Rose would want to know so that next time, she gets a gift you'd like."

Zoe's hands start to sweat. Even the thought of having such an awkward conversation with Aunt Rose is making her anxious.

"I bet there's another way to communicate this with Aunt Rose," Zoe's mother tells her. "Maybe instead of focusing on what you don't like, you can focus on what you do like."

And suddenly, Zoe has a great idea! She calls Aunt Rose to thank her for the sweater, then asks if they can go shopping together next week. Aunt Rose agrees, and both are looking forward to spending time together.

At the mall, Zoe points out all of the clothes, shoes, and accessories that catch her eye. She tells Aunt Rose how she would combine certain pieces and what kind of effect she's going for. Her aunt loves hearing her talk about her approach to fashion. By the end of the day, Aunt Rose has a much better idea of Zoe's sense of style—and she knows Zoe's going to *love* her next gift!

Are You Standing Up
for Yourself?

1. **You get to the bus stop early so you can grab a seat in the front (if you're in the back, you get motion sickness). When you get on the bus, a girl puts her hand on the only empty seat in the front and says, "Sorry, this seat is saved—my friend's getting on in a few stops." What do you say to her?**

   A. "Saving seats isn't allowed."
   B. "I get motion sickness if I'm not up here. Maybe you and your friend can sit in the back?"
   C. "Oh, cool. How about I sit here until we get to her stop?"
   D. "Omigod, I'm so sorry! I'll go to the back."

2. **Your best friend is in a bad mood today. At lunch, you crack a joke to cheer her up, and she snaps at you! You take a deep breath and respond . . .**

A. "Sheesh. I was just trying to be nice."
B. "Hey, I didn't deserve that. Is something wrong? You seem upset."
C. "I'm going to sit at another table. Text me when you're feeling better."
D. "I'm sorry! Is there anything I can do to make you feel better?"

3. **You can't stand scary movies. They always give you nightmares. And all of your friends know this. But during a sleepover party, everyone wants to watch the new horror movie on Netflix. What do you do?**

A. I remind them about my strict "no scary movie" policy. It's not happening!
B. I joke about waking them all up later when I have a nightmare, then suggest a few other options to watch instead.
C. I shrug and play games on my phone with my earbuds in while they watch.

D. I don't want to ruin everyone's fun, so I watch it with my pillow over my head most of the time.

4. **There's a kid in one of your classes who's been making a lot of unwanted comments about your appearance, especially your new glasses. You've already asked him to leave you alone, and that didn't work. The next time he does it, what's your plan?**

A. Call him out in front of the whole class, including the teacher.

B. Talk to the teacher after class and ask her to intervene next time.

C. Sit on the other side of the classroom. If I'm not near him, maybe he'll forget about me.

D. Give up. I already told him to leave me alone, and it only made things worse.

5. **One of your friends is about to have a birthday, and, as a surprise, your other friends want everyone to chip in to get her a new bike. It's a thoughtful gift ... but there's no way you can afford it. What do you do?**

A. Tell my friends I don't have that kind of money and ask if we can find a less expensive (but still nice!) group gift.

B. Drop a few hints that a bike is out of my price range. If no one picks up on it, I'll see if I can do a few extra chores to earn the money.

C. Let my friends know I already bought a birthday gift, so I won't take part in the group gift. Then I'll get her a present I can afford.

D. Accept the fact that I don't have friends anymore, because obviously they're all going to hate me when I ruin the group gift.

6. **Your little sister is starting to get into fashion—but she's totally copying all your looks! You think it's cute, but also kinda cringey when you both show up to school dressed almost identically. How do you deal?**

A. I'll talk to her about how fashion is all about individuality. Then I'll offer to go shopping with her and help her figure out her own sense of style.

B. I'll tell her I'm flattered she likes my style so much, then suggest she experiment with copying other fashion icons she admires.

C. I'll just change my look a little. It's fun to shake things up sometimes, anyway.

D. If I tell her, I might hurt her feelings, and then she'll cry and it'll turn into a whole thing. I'll ask our mom to talk to her about it.

7. **Your parents have a strict rule about not hanging out at a friend's house unless there's an adult present. When a new friend invites you and a bunch of other kids over after school, you want to say yes—but you know her parents won't be there. What do you do?**

A. Be honest and tell her I appreciate the invite, but I'm not allowed.

B. Tell her I want to come but I have to check with my parents. I know what they'll say, but it'll buy me some time . . .

C. Make up a lie about already having other plans.

D. Say yes, then spend the entire time stressing about how much trouble I'll be in when my parents find out.

Mostly As: I'm a Super Self-Advocate!

When it comes to standing up for yourself, you're aces! You've got your priorities straight, you know your own boundaries, and you're not afraid to enforce them. Just remember that others have feelings and boundaries too. Consider their situation and intent before you go on the attack.

Mostly Bs: I've Got My Own Back (Usually)

You know what you're about—and for the most part, everyone else knows it too. Most of the time, you're not afraid to draw a line in the sand. But every once in a while, you might find yourself reluctant—or even afraid—to speak up. It happens! Talk it out with a trusted friend or family member. They've got your back too.

Mostly Cs: I'm Chill, It's No Biggie

You don't sweat the small stuff. Hey, it's how you keep your stress levels so low! And while that's awesome, your gut will tell you when something happens that you can't let slide. In those moments, standing up for yourself is worth a little temporary anxiety.

Mostly Ds: Do I Have to Speak Up? Really?

You're very empathetic. The fact that you care so much about others' feelings makes you a truly amazing person—but sometimes, you've got to be your own best friend. After all, your happiness is just as important as anyone else's, right? And hey, bonus: seeing you stand up for yourself will totally make your friends and family happy too!

ASK THE EXPERT

Cara Goodwin, PhD
Child Psychologist

Do you have any tips for asking for help from a teacher? It feels awkward sometimes.
—Grace, 12, Maryland, USA

It can feel *so* awkward asking for help! It's hard to admit that there is something you can't do on your own. It's helpful to remember that we all have to ask for help sometimes and that asking for help means you are smart enough to know that one person can't know everything. To make it a little less awkward, set up a time to talk to your teacher one-on-one, which often feels more comfortable than doing so in front of other classmates. Then have a clear idea of exactly what you want to ask. Remember that teachers love questions because it shows that you care about what you are learning.

I have a giant social studies project that counts for half of my grade and involves standing up in front of the class and doing a presentation. I'm so nervous. Please help!
—Ellie, 11, California, USA

Oh, wow—that is a lot of pressure. I can see why you would be nervous. There are ways to make giving a presentation less nerve-racking. Let's break it down step by step. First, make sure you know the material really well. Use a study method that has worked for you in the past, like testing yourself with flash cards or writing a script. If you have done your prep work, you are more likely to feel confident when talking about the subject. Second, it helps to practice as much as possible before the big event. You can practice a few times by yourself and then in front of your family or friends. Finally, be careful about how you think and talk to yourself about the presentation. Thinking things like "I'm going to screw up" or "Everyone will think I'm dumb" will only make you more nervous! Try to use positive self-talk, like "I've got this" or "I've worked hard. I know I can do this."

CHAPTER 4

STICKY SITUATIONS

Brace yourself—things are about to get cringey.

Managing your worries when it comes to introducing yourself, trying new things, or asking someone for help is one thing. Deep down, we know that more often than not, everything will turn out okay. What about those times when things are anything *but* okay?

Like when you spend a lunch period talking to your crush, only to realize you had spinach stuck in your teeth the whole time?

Or when a friend says something that really hurts your feelings or vice versa?

Or when you swing for a home run, only to get a third strike and lose the game for your team?

Ouch. It's totally acceptable to dive into bed and hide under your blankets for a few days, right?

Well, sure. But sooner or later, you're going to have to confront these sticky situations. Sometimes, there's no avoiding a little bit of anxiety.

The funny thing is that hiding from the conflict can actually make us even *more* anxious. It builds up in our minds until we're basically panicking.

If you know how to deal with these situations, that means you can diffuse the tension. You can start to *relax*. So let's talk about how to deal with awkward moments, thorny conversations, rumors, mistakes, and more.

WHAT TO DO WHEN YOU HAVE A SUPER EMBARRASSING MOMENT

Embarrassing moments aren't the end of the world . . . but they sure feel like it sometimes! Your chest is so tight it's hard to breathe. Your stomach is churning so much you're worried you might lose your lunch. Your face is on fire. That's because feeling embarrassed activates your body's fight-or-flight response. Your heart rate speeds up, and your body releases adrenaline, which speeds up your breathing—and causes the blood vessels in your face to dilate. That means more blood flows to your cheeks, and you blush.

If you experience anxiety in other areas of your life, this feeling might sound very familiar to you. But even people who don't have mental health issues have anxiety-inducing embarrassing moments now and then. We can probably think of a few people we know who never seem to be embarrassed.

Here's a little secret: it's not because embarrassing things don't happen to them. It's because of how they *react*.

And the good news is, you can control your reaction. Next time you find yourself having a cringey moment, try this:

* **Laugh it off.** The best way to deal with embarrassment is to find the humor in it. Be real—if someone else's soda can exploded when they opened it, wouldn't you be giggling? It's okay to laugh at yourself! Plus, it breaks the tension and helps you relax.

* **Admit it**. Yes, that's right—admit you're embarrassed. Since everyone knows what embarrassment feels like, most people are really empathetic about it. They can understand how you feel. Simply saying something like "Well, that was embarrassing!" acknowledges how you feel and encourages others to commiserate with you.

* **Move on.** An embarrassing moment might feel like it goes on forever, but it's just one moment. In reality, other people might not have even noticed. You don't need to pretend it didn't happen, but you also don't have to wallow in it. If you act like it wasn't a big deal, it won't be.

The Replay (and How to Stop It)

One day at school, you walk out of the restroom with toilet paper stuck to your shoe. Worse, you don't even notice it until a kid points it out during lunch! It's *so* embarrassing, but in the moment, you were able to laugh about it and move on quickly. Success!

But that night, you're lying in bed reading a book, totally minding your own business, and the memory resurfaces. In your mind, you watch the scene play out over . . . and over . . . and over again. *Make it stop!*

This is super common. Our brains love to pick through all our memories, choose the worst ones, and play them like a movie stuck on repeat. The worst part is, our body reacts the same way—blushing, shallow breathing, even tears! Our brain is trying to help us out so we learn something from the experience. But it feels like we're reliving the moment. So how do we hit that mental stop button? Well, we don't. Not at first.

* *Sit with it.* Trying to ignore the memory almost never works. Instead, allow yourself to focus on it for a minute. Feel the feels.

* *Make it objective.* Your brain is amazingly creative. It will turn a little moment into a BIG one. But really think about it . . . was the *entire* cafeteria laughing at you? Or was it just your friends who were giggling?

* *Acknowledge the reality.* "I saw the toilet paper on my shoe and felt really embarrassed. My friends giggled as I pulled it off. I threw it away and went back to my seat. Then we started talking about the game tomorrow. The whole thing lasted only about half a minute."

* *Breathe deeply.* Taking a few nice, long breaths is scientifically proven to help your body relax. As you exhale, imagine that you're blowing the embarrassing memory like a bubble that drifts farther and farther away until it's gone.

* *Be realistic.* You're thinking about this more than anyone. Do you remember what you wore yesterday? Probably so. What about what your best friend wore? Your math teacher? The girl next to you in gym class? Probably not. Everyone is way more focused on themselves and their own embarrassing moments.

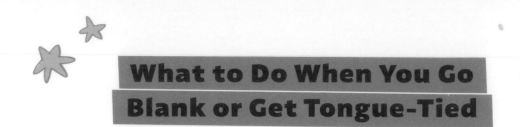

What to Do When You Go Blank or Get Tongue-Tied

Your PE coach is explaining how to use the weight machines in the gym. As you watch her demonstrate the bench press, you think of a question and raise your hand.

When your coach finishes, she smiles at you. "Yes? Do you have a question?"

You open your mouth . . . and your mind goes totally blank. Whatever that question was, it's *gone*.

"Um . . . I forgot!"

Your coach moves on to the dumbbells. And suddenly you remember your question! Your hand shoots up again, and when your coach nods, you take a deep breath.

"With the bench press, how do we know when . . . like, if I wanted to add more weights . . . how much could I . . . "

It's such a simple question in your mind. But it's like your tongue is tripping over every word until it all sounds like nonsense. People with ADHD might experience this sensation more often than others—but it can happen to anyone.

It's hard to predict when we're going to have these moments. And even though they're usually no big deal, they can *feel* like a big deal—and their unpredictability can cause us a ton of anxiety. Think about it: next time you want to ask your PE coach a question, your brain will probably say, "Whoa, hang on . . . remember what happened last time? That was so cringey. Better just not ask at all."

Don't let these little mind-blank, tongue-tied moments stop you from asking questions or trying new things. The best thing to do is learn how to handle them so you feel prepared when they pop up. Here are some things to keep in mind:

* **Give it a beat.** When your mind goes blank or your tongue gets tied, it's normal to panic. But panicking only makes it harder for us to say what we want to say. So, take a moment—and a nice, deep breath—before you go on.

* **Ask for a little time.** Don't just mumble "never mind." Everyone will understand if you say, "Sorry, I just went totally blank . . . come back to me later?"

* **Mentally rewind.** While the attention (and pressure) is off you, try to think back a few minutes. What were you thinking about? What were you looking at? What were others saying? More often than not, your thought will return—and you'll know exactly how to phrase it this time.

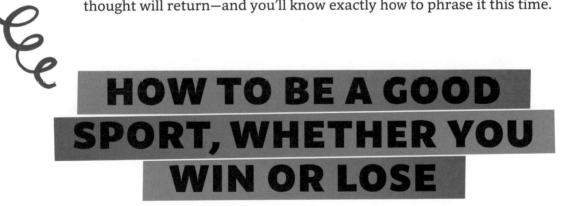

HOW TO BE A GOOD SPORT, WHETHER YOU WIN OR LOSE

Who doesn't love to win? Whether it's bowling, a track meet, a board game, or scoring the lead in your school musical, coming out on top is pretty much guaranteed to make you feel great.

But of course, sometimes things don't work out that way. You might practice your heart out for band auditions only to get last chair. An unexpected injury

could cost your soccer team the championship. You campaigned for student council treasurer for weeks only to lose to your rival.

It's okay to feel sad or upset about these outcomes. In fact, it's healthy to acknowledge those feelings! After all, you're bound to learn something from all of this that will better prepare you for whatever competition comes your way next.

But it's *not* okay to be a bad sport about losing. What does that mean? It's basically when you use your negative emotions as an excuse for negative behavior. You can feel angry, but you don't have to act rude. You can feel disappointed, but you don't have to act disrespectfully. You can feel hurt, but you don't have to insult the victor.

Sometimes, that's a lot easier said than done in the moment. Next time you find yourself watching someone else claim the victory you wanted so badly, put the following tips into practice:

* ✱ **Cool off.** If you're feeling really heated about the loss, temporarily remove yourself from the situation until you've got those emotions in check.

* **Feel proud of your efforts.** Win or lose, you worked hard and accomplished a lot. Losing doesn't take any of that away from you.
* **Accept the loss.** Denying it or making excuses will just make you look like a sore loser. A good sport can accept defeat with grace and humility.
* **Congratulate the winner.** Shake their hand and offer a smile. It's the respectful thing to do. Plus, it will make you feel better!
* **Think of it as an opportunity.** Failure is a part of life. The most successful people in the world treat their failures as a chance to learn and improve.

Remember that it's totally possible to be a bad sport even when you win. Bragging, rubbing your victory in the loser's face, and showing off are a surefire way to show everyone you might not have deserved that win after all. Show your competitors the same courtesy you hope they would show you.

HOW TO APOLOGIZE WHEN YOU HURT SOMEONE'S FEELINGS

"I'm sorry."

It's two little words. So why is the idea of apologizing so awkward sometimes? When you hurt someone, you know you owe her an apology. But before long, your brain is like "Maybe she didn't even hear me" or "Maybe she already forgot about it."

But think about it—the last time someone hurt your feelings, did you forget about it? Probably not!

Ignoring a problem won't make it go away. Admitting that you did or said something that hurt someone you care about might feel totally yuck in the moment. But you'll feel so much better once you say those two magic words.

Picture This

Courtni loves making people laugh—and she's great at it. Her dream is to become a stand-up comedian, and she sees every day as an opportunity to try out a new joke. Her best friend, Priya, is her number one fan.

When Priya shows up to school with bright green rubber bands in her braces, Courtni immediately thinks of a funny joke.

"Don't worry, Priya, I bet they make a special toothpaste for moldy teeth!"

It gets a laugh from everyone in class . . . except Priya, who offers Courtni a tight-lipped smile as she sits down at her desk. Courtni's stomach flip-flops uncomfortably.

At lunch, she can't help but notice that Priya keeps hiding her mouth behind her sandwich.

"Hey, about what I said earlier," Courtni says. "You know that was just a joke, right?"

"Yeah, I know." Priya replies. She doesn't seem to be mad.

After school, the girls chat about their favorite show as they get on the bus. Courtni is pretty sure Priya has already forgotten about the moldy teeth joke. So there's nothing to apologize for . . . or is there?

Empathy is key when it comes to apologies. That's when you try to understand how another person is feeling. How would you feel if you were Priya? Do you think she'd feel better if Courtni said she was sorry about the joke? When you hurt someone's feelings—whether you meant to or not—it damages the trust between you. A heartfelt apology is the best way to start repairing that damage.

Remember, making mistakes is normal! We all do it. The most important thing is taking responsibility by acknowledging and learning from our mistakes.

3 Steps to a Heartfelt Apology

Even when you want to apologize, it can be hard to know what to say and how to say it. These three tips will help!

1. *Make it quick.* You don't have to recount everything you did or said in detail—you both know that already. Get right to the "I'm sorry."

2. *No excuses.* You didn't mean to hurt your friend's feelings, but the point is, you did. Don't spend time explaining your actions and acting defensive. The whole point of apologizing is to let them know you understand why your actions were hurtful, you regret it, and you'll avoid doing it again.

3. *Give her time.* Apologizing is up to you. But forgiveness isn't. If your friend doesn't forgive you right away, that's okay! Be patient and do everything you can to show her she can trust you.

What to Do When a Friend Hurts Your Feelings

Trust is one of the most important elements in any friendship. Think about the very first time you met your best friend. Did you instantly spill all your deepest, darkest secrets? You probably got to know each other and built trust first.

That's why it's extra tough when a friend hurts our feelings—whether they mean to or not. It feels almost like a betrayal—and in some cases, it is. Our trust is broken, and it might take a while for it to heal. We can't control what our friends do or how they behave once they realize they've hurt our feelings. But we *can* control how we react to it. Next time you find yourself stung by a friend's words or actions, try this:

* **Take time to cool off.** Sometimes when we're hurt, we feel angry too. That's completely normal. But it's easy to lash out when you're angry. You might even say or do something you don't really mean. A little time and a few nice, deep breaths can help you get into a more rational headspace.

* **Consider your friend's perspective.** More often than not, our friends don't intend to hurt us. Your friend's actions or words might have been careless. Maybe they were under pressure in the moment. Maybe they were simply in a bad mood—it happens to all of us! That doesn't excuse hurtful behavior. But it can provide a little context and help you understand why they did what they did.

* **Talk to your friend.** It can be very tempting to avoid this step. After all, telling someone they hurt your feelings is pretty awkward. Often, we end up venting to our other friends

instead. That might make you feel better temporarily, but it can do more harm than good in the long run. The best thing to do is calmly discuss the issue with your friend.

* **Explain what they did.** Imagine you promised a friend you would loan her your calculator for her math test because hers is broken. You plan to meet in the hall between classes, but you get totally distracted and forget. For the rest of the day, your friend gives you the cold shoulder, and you don't know why. Wouldn't you rather your friend simply remind you of your promise so you can apologize? It's best to be upfront about what your friend said or did that hurt your feelings rather than dropping hints or staying silent.

* **Tell them why you feel hurt.** Let's say your friend made a comment about your new haircut that hurt your feelings. Your feelings are valid. But that doesn't mean your friend intended to insult you! Explain why the comment stung, and give your friend the chance to explain what they meant.

* **Hear them out.** You might be surprised by your friend's reasons for their actions. Or maybe they have no excuse at all. Either way, you won't know unless you give them a chance to tell you their side. Once you do, you can both look for a resolution together.

Remember that forgiveness is always an option. When a friend deliberately hurts us, it can be tough to move forward. If your friend apologizes, it's up to you whether or not you choose to forgive—and whether your friendship can go back to the way it was.

WHAT TO DO WHEN YOU MAKE A BIG MISTAKE

Yikes.

A girl was getting teased during gym class for her clumsiness, and you joined in.

You promised your brother you'd go to his first Little League game, but then you blew it off because your best friend wanted to hang out.

You panicked during a quiz and glanced at your classmate's answers . . . and copied them.

In other words, you just made a HUGE mistake. Now what? When you make a mistake, your immediate instinct might be to pretend it didn't happen at all. Your brain immediately starts making excuses. That girl probably didn't mind the teasing. Your brother was too busy with the game to notice your absence. Your classmate didn't see you copy their answers—you think—so hey, no harm done. Right?

Wrong.

Pretending your mistake never happened will only make you feel worse over time. After all, you're lying to yourself—and who likes being lied to?

On the flip side, you might feel panicked after making a mistake. You have to

fix it *right now!* The problem is that we're pretty much never at our best when we're in panic mode. When you're feeling this way, you might end up making a big mistake even *bigger*.

That's why the first thing you should do when you make a mistake is stay calm. You might try taking a few deep breaths, for example. Remind yourself that no matter what, this mistake isn't the end of the world. Clear your head so you can focus on what to do next.

Then be honest about what you've done—not just to yourself, but to anyone who was affected by your mistake. Reach out to the girl who was bullied and tell her you're sorry. Apologize to your brother for missing the game. Set a calendar reminder to study for your next quiz and vow not to cheat again.

Finally, consider what you can learn from your mistake. Think of it as a learning opportunity! What will you do next time? Stand up for the girl in your gym class? Invite your best friend to come to your brother's game with you? Get a new planner so you don't forget to study for your next quiz? You can turn this negative into a positive if you think about it as a chance to grow and become an even better person.

THE INS AND OUTS OF RUMORS, SECRETS, AND GOSSIP

Here's the thing about gossip: everyone does it at some point. We might genuinely think the rumor we're spreading is true. Or maybe we don't care—it's a juicy secret, and we want to share it with others! We aren't always proud of it, especially if it ends up hurting someone else.

So why do we gossip in the first place?

There's actually science behind this. In fact, researchers who study gossip point out that it isn't always a negative thing. Really, it's just people talking about another person who isn't present.

"Cara had a big argument with her parents this morning. That's why she's been in such a weird mood today."

"Poor Cara! Maybe we can cheer her up at lunch."

Is this gossip? Yes. But is it mean or negative? No! This sounds like a conversation between two people who are concerned about their friend.

Researchers found that gossip is usually neutral, and negative only 15 percent of the time. There's a reason humans have always engaged in gossip—many reasons, actually! It's a way for us to bond and feel close with others. It helps us share social information. It promotes cultural learning. And let's be real . . . it's often entertaining.

But gossip isn't always kind. Rumors can cause a lot of harm, whether the secret is true or not.

"Did you hear about April? Apparently, she laughed so hard in gym, she wet her pants!"

"Ew, gross! I have to sit next to her in math next period."

In this case, the gossip about April is obviously negative. And it might not even be true!

Oops . . . I Spread a Rumor, and Now I Feel Bad About It. What Do I Do?

If you find out the rumor is false, the first thing you can do is let whoever you shared the information with know that it isn't true. That will help stop the rumor from spreading even more.

If you still aren't sure if the rumor is true, or if you know it's true but it's private and could be harmful to someone, make an effort to ask those you shared the information with not to spread it. They may or may not choose to listen, but it doesn't hurt to try.

Next comes the hard part: talking to the person who was the subject of the gossip. Offer an apology and ask them if they want to know what the gossip was about. Remember, it doesn't matter if the information was true or not.

Finally, don't expect forgiveness right away. Give the person a little time and space to deal with it, and ask if there's anything else you can do to make things right in the meantime.

I Just Found Out There's a Rumor About Me Going Around! Now What?!

It never feels good to realize you're the subject of gossip. It's okay to feel sad, hurt, or even angry. But it's also not the best emotional state to be in when making decisions. Your instinct might be to immediately confront anyone who participated in the gossip, but give yourself a little time to cool down before you do. In the meantime, try these options:

✳ **Find your support group.** This means friends and adults that you trust. Talk to them about the gossip and how it's making you feel, and allow them to offer their support.

✳ **Confront the gossipers.** After you have cooled down and know you can stay calm, let them know that their actions hurt your feelings. Give them a chance to apologize, then decide whether or not you forgive them.

✳ **Report bullies.** If the gossip is harmful and you feel you are being bullied, find an adult and let them know what's going on.

✳ **Avoid the urge to retaliate.** When someone hurts us, our instinct sometimes is to hurt them right back. But this kind of situation can easily escalate and get out of control—and in the end, it only results in even more hurt feelings.

* **Engage in self-care.** This might mean manicures with your friends, a solo dance party in your bedroom, or a few hours playing your favorite video game. Gossip hurts, so do what you can to help yourself heal!

HELP! I TOTALLY FORGOT ABOUT . . .

It happens to all of us sooner or later. Maybe it's a big geometry test, or your best friend's birthday, or something you borrowed from a classmate. It's super important—you even wrote it down in your planner—and then you completely forgot all about it.

Oops!

Your anxiety skyrockets as your brain immediately starts to catastrophize. Will you fail the test? Will your friend be furious? Where is that thing you borrowed—did you lose it?!

Before you know it, you're coming up with excuses and looking for a way to explain things so that it's not your fault. That's normal! After all, we don't mean to do harm when we forget something important. We just . . . forgot.

The thing is, it *is* our fault. And taking responsibility for whatever happens next is pretty much always going to work out better than coming up with a little white lie. The next time you forget something important, here's how to handle it:

- ✳ **Own up.** Admit that you forgot—with zero excuses. That means telling your teacher you forgot to study, acknowledging that you forgot your friend's birthday, and admitting to your classmate that you forgot to return what you borrowed.

- ✳ **Apologize (if necessary).** Sometimes, the only person you owe an apology to is yourself. But if someone else might have been hurt by your forgetfulness—like your friend on her birthday—a simple "I'm sorry" can help undo the damage.

- ✳ **Explain how you're going to change.** How will you avoid forgetting this in the future? For example, show your teacher how you've entered the next big test in your phone calendar so you get an alert the day before.

- ✳ **Offer a solution.** Will your teacher allow you to take a retest? Can you treat your friend to laser tag (her favorite) or bake her a batch of fudge brownies? Can you return the borrowed item to your classmate ASAP?

Forgetting important things can be frustrating, embarrassing, and stressful. But owning up to your mistake will go a long way toward building trust with anyone you may have let down.

What's Your Communication Style?

1. **At your last band rehearsal, a fellow percussionist asked to borrow a pair of drumsticks. You said yes, but made it clear you needed them back tomorrow before the concert. The next day, he shows up without your sticks. What do you do?**

   A. Tell him to find me another pair of sticks in the next 10 minutes, or else!
   B. Start asking around to see if anyone has an extra pair.
   C. Shrug and tell him it's fine—but then not talk to him for at least a week.
   D. Tell him I'm disappointed, then ask him to help me find another pair before the concert.

2. **There's a new girl at your school, and she seems really shy. You overhear a group of kids whispering about her, and the things they're saying aren't very nice—and** probably aren't even true. How would you handle it?

   A. I'd march up to them and tell them starting rumors is really mean.
   B. I wouldn't say anything. But next time I saw the new girl, I would introduce myself and try to make her feel welcome.
   C. I'd give them all a dirty look and ignore them until they started treating the new girl better.
   D. I'd ask them if they've actually gotten to know her yet. If they say no, I'd suggest we all try to get to know her better instead of spreading rumors about her.

3. **At lunch, a friend accidentally bumps into your tray, dumping your entire lunch into your lap. Everyone starts laughing as you sit there covered in french fries, chicken fingers, and milk—and today of all days, you were wearing a brand-new skirt you love.**

Your friend apologizes profusely. How do you react?

A. "You should be more careful. I'm not sure these stains are ever going to come out!"
B. "It's okay. The stain will come out."
C. "Guess I need to buy a new skirt. Great."
D. "No worries, I know it was an accident. I love this skirt, though—would you mind helping me try to clean up in the restroom?"

4. **You spent the entire weekend working on a big essay, and you're proud of it. So when your teacher hands it back with a C, you're really upset. Especially because she didn't leave a lot of feedback, so you don't understand why you got such a low score. What do you do?**

A. Raise my hand and ask that she explain exactly what I did wrong.
B. Nothing. I guess I'll try harder next time.
C. Stop trying so hard. Clearly nothing I do is good enough for this teacher, so why bother?
D. Stop by her desk after class and ask if we can meet after school to discuss my grade.

5. **You're having a blast with your new theater group. But some of the kids keep pressuring you to hang out after rehearsal in the woods behind the community center. You're not comfortable with that—it's usually getting dark out by then. You've told them you don't want to several times, but today they push you *again*. You're annoyed you have to say no one more time. How does it come out?**

A. "Would you guys lay off? I said no like a thousand times."
B. "I'm really, really sorry, but I can't go. Please don't hate me!"
C. "Do you guys think no means yes? Is it Opposite Day?"
D. "Thanks for the invitation, but I've already told you guys I'm not interested. I'd appreciate it if you stopped asking."

6. **Your friends forget your birthday. It's never happened before, but today is one of those days where everyone is rushed and frantic. You know it's just a mistake, but you can't help feeling a little hurt. By the end of the day, you feel like you might explode if you don't say something. What would you do?**

A. I'd tell them how awful they made me feel and point out that I've never forgotten any of their birthdays.

B. I'd go to my room and listen to some music. They'll probably remember tomorrow.

C. I'd let it slide. But next time it's one of their birthdays, I hope they don't expect anything from me.

D. I'd be honest and tell them I know everyone is busy, but today was my birthday, and it hurt my feelings that no one remembered.

7. **You just started a new school, and you've already made a few friends! One invites you over to hang out on Saturday, and you're super excited. But then she suggests you film a dance together to post on TikTok. You like making videos, but you're not comfortable dancing in front of anyone, much less the whole Internet. How would you deal?**

A. I'd say that I'm happy to learn the dance with her, but I definitely don't want to put it on TikTok.

B. I'd probably just do it and hope not that many people would see it.

C. I'd make something up, like saying I twisted my ankle and can't dance right now.

D. I'd say I'm not much of a dancer, but I'd be happy to film her dancing.

Answers

Mostly As: Waging War with Words

You have strong beliefs and aren't afraid to express them. That's awesome! But this particular style of communication is known as *aggressive*. You don't have to compromise your ideas and opinions—just consider your tone and the way you deliver your message. If you find yourself raising your voice and not listening to the other person, it might be a good idea to take a few minutes to cool down before continuing the conversation.

Mostly Bs: Keeping the Peace

You don't like conflict—you want everyone to be happy. And while that's great, this *passive* style of communication can make the conflict worse over the long term. After all, the longer you keep your opinions and feelings bottled up, the more likely they'll spill over one day. Don't be afraid to express yourself to your friends and family. Most likely, this will diffuse the tension rather than create more of it.

Mostly Cs: Indirect Conflict

You always let everyone know exactly how you're feeling or what you're thinking. You just don't use words to do it. Relying on things like body language or sarcasm to make your point is what's called a *passive aggressive* communication style. If you have something to say, don't be afraid to say it—no hinting or sarcasm required!

Mostly Ds: Calm, Clear Communication

You know your opinion matters, but you also respect the ideas of others. That's why your *assertive* communication style is known as the healthiest! Others can see you're someone who speaks her mind, and that you admire those who do the same.

ASK THE EXPERT

Cara Goodwin, PhD
Child Psychologist

How can I feel more comfortable in crowded places?
–Vivian, 11, California, USA

Feeling nervous or uncomfortable in crowded places is normal. But simply avoiding all crowded places may make your anxiety worse in the long term. To become more comfortable with crowds, start with the least overwhelming situation, like visiting a museum on a weekday morning, and work your way up to more and more overwhelming situations. Practice some coping skills to make these situations easier to tolerate, such as deep breathing, closing your eyes and visualizing a calm place, or reminding yourself that you are safe. You can also use a skill called mindfulness, which means focusing on the present moment. For example, you might concentrate on the sensation of breathing in and out, or count the number of steps you take.

I made a big mistake, and I can't stop thinking about it. Do you have any advice for how to move on?
—Charlotte, 11, London, UK

We all make mistakes. And we all have trouble not fixating on those mistakes. It may not help to just try to stop thinking about it since our brains can't really turn off in this way. Instead, try letting yourself think about the mistake and feel any emotions you have related to it (embarrassment, anger, or sadness). Then try to reframe the event by thinking about it in a different way. Did you learn something from it? Could the mistake have been a lot worse? You can also think about what you would say to a friend who made the same mistake. You probably wouldn't say that their life was over! You would probably tell them not to be so hard on themselves and that everyone messes up sometimes. Although it may not seem like it now, in time, your big feelings about this mistake will fade. Be patient with yourself.

CHAPTER 5

TOUGH STUFF

Let's face it—everyone's social life has ups and downs. And you never know when those "downs" are going to strike. You're excited to start a new school year when suddenly you find out your best friend since kindergarten is moving away. Or maybe your basketball team is heading for the state championship, but then the star forward gets a knee injury right before the big game. Or a friend's parent passes away and she's grieving, and you realize you have no idea what to do or say to help.

Now what? Suddenly, your whole life feels off-kilter, and you don't know how to act. Your anxiety comes raging back worse than ever. You feel like all that hard work you did on making new friends, trying new things, and setting healthy boundaries was just totally undone. Now you have to start all over, right?

WHAT THE REBELS SAY

"Doing art projects helps me feel less anxious."
—Naomi, 8, New Mexico, USA

Wrong! Managing social anxiety and maintaining a healthy social life is a journey, not a destination. And like any trip, it's important to think about what you're going to pack. In this case, you'll want to prepare by packing tools and techniques to help you manage the tough stuff when it happens.

In this chapter, we'll talk about everything you need to handle those moments when it feels like the world is imploding.

HOW TO HANDLE BULLYING

What exactly is bullying? It's one of those things we all know about, but sometimes, it's hard to define. Is whispering about a friend behind her back considered bullying? What about ignoring a kid in gym class because you think he's annoying?

According to StopBullying.gov, the act of bullying is "being mean to another kid over and over again." This might mean physical violence like hitting, slapping, pinching, or shoving. It can also include threatening to hurt someone physically, even if you don't actually intend to act on your words. Bullying includes teasing and saying mean things about another kid. And it can also include ignoring or leaving kids out on purpose.

That's just in person! All of this can happen online too, and it's called cyberbullying. Joining in with a lot of other kids to make rude comments on someone's Instagram post is cyberbullying. Sharing video of someone on TikTok without their permission to embarrass them? Yup, that's cyberbullying. Basically, being mean to someone through texts, emails, and social media all falls under the bullying umbrella.

Bullying can have a really negative effect on our physical, mental, and emotional health. It can make us feel anxious and scared to the point of getting sick. It's pretty much the worst! That's why Rebel Girls know how to recognize bullying—and how to handle it.

What Do I Do When I See Someone Being Bullied?

Watching a bully pick on someone can make us feel a whole lot of things: fear, pity, even depression. Often, we want to stand up to them . . . but what if the bully decides to make us the new target?

In some situations, it's great to stand up to a bully. For example, imagine you're in a crowded hallway between classes. You spot a bully taunting another girl at her locker, and she's crying. Some kids are laughing, but a lot of kids look like you feel—upset but too afraid to speak up.

The thing is, often it takes only one person speaking up to turn things around. If you simply say, "Hey, that's not very nice! Leave her alone," your bravery will spread. Other kids will chime in with their support, and the bully will be outnumbered.

That said, if you feel unsafe around a bully, you definitely don't have to confront them yourself. Another option is to find the nearest adult right away and alert them to what's going on so they can intervene. Later, find the bully's victim and ask them if they're okay. Kids who get bullied often feel isolated and alone. Taking a minute to check on them and offer support can help them heal.

What Do I Do If I'm Being Bullied?

Getting targeted by a bully is a stressful experience. No one deserves that, including you! The kid picking on you is likely dealing with their own issues. Maybe they're getting bullied too, and they're taking it out on you. Maybe they just want to look cool in front of their friends. Regardless of the reason, none of that is an excuse for their actions. There are a few different strategies you can try when dealing with a bully.

* **Stay calm and tell them to stop.** Bullies want to see a reaction, like crying or blushing. Those things are really hard to control. But if you appear unbothered and simply say, "Please don't do that again," you might be surprised at the result. If you aren't giving the bully the reaction they want, they're way more likely to back off.

* **Laugh with them.** Of course, this isn't appropriate in every situation. But if someone is teasing you in front of a group, they're usually trying to entertain the others. If you're the first to laugh, the other kids present will be laughing with you, not at you. It's a subtle shift that takes the power away from the bully.

* **Find an adult.** It's not tattling—it's asking for help. And remember what we talked about in chapter 3? Asking for help is brave, a sign of maturity, and sometimes scary—but you can do it! A trusted teacher,

coach, counselor, or parent can help you process your feelings and come up with a plan to deal with the bullying.

* **Think twice about what you share online.** When you post a photo or video, it's out there forever. Don't share anything that you wouldn't want a potential bully to get their hands on. Double-check your privacy settings to control who gets to see your posts.

* **Take care with texts.** Just like social media posts, texts often can't be deleted. Be mindful of what you text to friends and in group chats.

I Want to Do More!

Here's the thing about bullying: kids know more about it than adults, because they are the ones experiencing it. Bullies often wait until there are no adults

around to act. For example, let's say your English class goes to the library every Friday. Although your teacher and the librarian are present, it's impossible to monitor every student as they roam the aisles. Every Friday, you see a bully target anyone who goes to get an encyclopedia in the back of the library. Your classmates all know this is happening, but your teacher doesn't—at least, not until YOU speak up.

Ask your school administration if there's a program or committee on school safety that you can join. If there isn't, start one. You can also write about bullying for your school's newspaper or website. These are all great ways to share what you know so that everyone can work together to address the problem.

WHAT TO DO WHEN SOMEONE IS SICK OR INJURED

When a friend or family member is sick or injured, it can cause a ton of anxiety. You want to make them feel better, but you're not sure how. Then there's all the uncertainty. How long will it take before they start feeling better? Plus, physical health issues often cause sadness and even depression. It's terrible to see someone you care about down in the dumps. But what can you do to cheer them up?

Before you know it, you're totally overwhelmed—and you're not the one who's sick! Now you're feeling guilty on top of everything else.

The truth is, you can't solve their health problems. But you can support them through this by following these steps:

* **Listen.** When we're sick or hurt, sometimes we just need to complain. This is especially true if the diagnosis or injury is new. Don't try and diminish their pain by saying things like "Well, it could be worse!" Allow them to vent their feelings and help them feel validated.

* **Ask them what you can do.** Some people love to be doted on when they're ill. Others want to be left alone. Find out what your friend or family member needs from you, and do it.

* **Research.** If you don't know a lot about their diagnosis or injury, look it up. You'll find tons of information online to help you better understand what they're going through, and it will help you figure out what to do—and what *not* to do. (For example, sending flowers to someone who is immunocompromised is actually a bad idea because they might contain mold and waterborne organisms.) Just make sure you are looking up information on reputable websites from hospitals or health-care organizations.

* **Change the subject.** When we've been dealing with a health issue for a while, sometimes we get tired of talking about it. While it's tempting to constantly ask an ill friend how she's feeling, chances are she's ready to talk about other stuff.

* **Reach out often.** Sometimes, we have to go weeks or even longer without seeing a sick or injured friend. But you don't want them to think you've forgotten them. Text or call regularly to see how they're doing and remind them you're still thinking about them. Even sending a funny GIF can make them smile and brighten their day.

HELP! IT'S AN EMERGENCY!

Emergency situations can cause a huge spike in anxiety. And that's okay—in fact, it can be a good thing! When we witness a medical emergency, like someone having a seizure, breaking their arm, or fainting, our body responds by giving us a rush of *adrenaline*. Adrenaline is a hormone that causes our heart to beat fast, makes us feel more alert, and raises the level of sugar in our blood so that we have energy to deal with the situation *fast*.

If you witness a medical emergency, the first thing to do is yell for help. The more people that come, the better—it takes the pressure off you, and everyone can work together to help the person having the emergency.

The next thing to do is call 911. If you don't have a phone, ask to borrow one (or ask someone nearby to make the call). Do your best to speak slowly and calmly on the call so the operator understands every word. Be prepared to explain what happened and let them know your location. The operator will likely give you instructions on what to do until help arrives.

After help has arrived, you might feel relieved—followed by another flood of worry. Remember how our brains like to play our embarrassing moments over and over again? It can do the same thing when we witness a traumatic event. The best thing to do is talk to sympathetic friends and family members about what happened. Telling the story out loud will help your body start to relax. If you're still buzzing with adrenaline, try taking a walk, riding your bike, or any other form of physical activity you enjoy. If you still

can't stop thinking about what happened after a couple of weeks, ask your grown-up if you should try talking to a therapist who can help you work through your feelings.

HOW TO SUPPORT A FRIEND GOING THROUGH A TOUGH TIME

Watching a friend go through a hard time can make us feel helpless. Seeing her sad makes us sad too. We want to do something to fix it, but we don't know what. Worse, there might not even be a way to fix it. So, how do we support her?

* **Let her tell you how to help.** Everyone is different, and there's no way to know exactly how to support someone in a way they'll appreciate unless we ask them. Listen to your friend and ask her exactly what she needs from you right now. If she needs a little alone time to process her feelings, don't feel hurt—respect her wishes and make sure to check in on her later.

* **Empathize without playing it down.** Often, our first reaction to hearing that a friend is having trouble is to think of a time when we were in a similar situation. For example, if your friend tried out for the school play and didn't land the role she wanted, it might remind you of when you didn't make the basketball team. That's called *empathizing*, and it allows you to better understand what your friend is feeling. Just make sure you don't downplay their problems. For example, saying, "At least you're still in the play! I didn't make the basketball team at all," isn't

helpful. It might make your friend feel as if her pain isn't valid, or it might frustrate her because that role meant a lot to her and you aren't recognizing that.

* **Sympathize without trying to fix it.** Telling someone "I'm so sorry you're going through this" is the best way to validate their feelings. But following it up by offering solutions is rarely as helpful as we think it will be. And the truth is, we all go through tough times that can't be "fixed." You might have a friend whose parents are getting divorced, or who just found out a grandparent is seriously ill. The best thing to do is be there for your friend and offer a shoulder to cry on.

* **Remind them you'll figure it out together.** When we see a friend upset, we often say things like "It'll all work out!" or "Everything will be okay!" Maybe it will, and maybe it won't . . . either way, those expressions aren't helpful in the moment. Instead, acknowledge that you don't know what will happen next—but make sure your friend knows you will be there for her no matter what.

How to Talk About It When You're Going Through a Tough Time

Life is full of ups and downs. And sometimes, those downs are *extra*. Like when a parent loses their job and the whole family suddenly has to deal with financial insecurity. Or when you fail a class despite your best efforts and realize there's a chance you might have to repeat a grade. Or when your best friend since kindergarten starts ghosting you and hanging out with a different crowd.

One of the hardest things about times like these is that we have little to no control. And that lack of control can make us feel super panicky. It's not like we can find another job for our parent, or force our teacher to pass us, or make our friend stop hanging out with those other kids.

There are lots of reasons we might resist talking to someone when we're having trouble with something. We might feel ashamed, embarrassed, or guilty. Maybe we just don't want to bother anyone with our worries. But our feelings are important, and sharing them with someone we trust can help us process them and figure out a way to move forward.

Most importantly, others want to help! You have friends and family who love and care about you. If you're struggling, they want to know so they can be there for you. After all, that's how you would feel if they were going through a hard time, right?

The cool thing is, you already have a *support system* in place. A support system is made up of the people in your life who care about you. This might include family, friends, classmates, teachers—and anyone else you trust. They're all here for you and ready to show compassion and support you when you need it. And right now, you *really* need it.

Still, it can be hard to tell someone what you're going through. Preparing beforehand can make you feel a lot more confident. Before you reach out to someone for support, think about exactly what you need right now. Do you want someone to help you figure out a solution to your problem? Did you just need to vent to someone? Be honest about your needs and allow your support system to do what they do best.

Picture This

Mallory is having a great school year. She's on the yearbook staff, and she's made lots of new friends, including a girl named Kayla. Plus, she's looking forward to her family's annual summer vacation at the lakehouse.

But a few weeks before the end of the semester, Mallory's parents tell her they're getting divorced. She is shocked and upset, especially when she realizes they won't be going to the lakehouse this summer. Their family vacations are over.

Mallory feels depressed. Her parents aren't fighting anymore, and they promise this is going to make things better, but she doesn't see how. She becomes withdrawn at school, and her closest friends notice. At a yearbook staff meeting, when they ask what's wrong, she doesn't tell them. It's not that she doesn't trust them. It's that they won't understand what she's going through. Plus, saying it out loud will make it all *real*.

The day the yearbook copies arrive, the whole staff gathers around excitedly to open the boxes. As they ooh and aah over their hard work, Mallory finds herself tearing up. She doesn't want to look at all the photos from back when she was happy. It's making her feel worse.

She excuses herself, and Kayla follows her. When Kayla asks what's wrong, it all comes pouring out. Through tears, Mallory tells her all about the divorce.

"And the worst part is, I can't stop thinking about our lakehouse vacation!" Mallory sobs. "Isn't that silly? It's just one week. Plus, I know my parents will be happier. I'm mad at them for not staying together, but at the same time, I feel selfish."

To her surprise, Kayla totally gets it. "My parents got divorced a few years ago," she tells Mallory. "It was really hard the first few months, but things got better."

Mallory listens as Kayla talks about her experience and what her family is like now. It's different, but not in a bad way. Mallory starts to imagine what her own family might look like in a year. They might not have the family vacation at the lakehouse anymore, but Mallory will have lots of new traditions with her mom and dad. She thanks her friend for talking to her. Sharing her feelings about the divorce was painful, but it really helped.

HOW TO HANDLE IT WHEN A FRIEND IS MOVING AWAY

Finding out a friend is moving can feel like a total gut punch. It's completely normal to feel sad or even angry. After all, think about all the stuff you won't get to do together now, like next year's big class trip to Six Flags, or going to high school together, or simply seeing each other every single day.

But remember, your friend is sad too. She might even be angry or resentful. And on top of all that, she's probably scared. She's going to start a new life at a new school. Everything is about to change.

The point is, it's okay to cry and feel upset. But focusing on cheering up your friend will help you feel better too. Here are some ideas that might help you both:

* **Brainstorm exciting new plans.** Okay, so you and your friend won't be science lab partners anymore, and Saturday night sleepovers are out of the picture. But maybe you can make a trip to see her over the summer for a week or two. Come up with a list of cool stuff to do in her new neighborhood—amusement parks, movie theaters, museums, anything goes!

* **Figure out how you'll keep in touch.** There are tons of ways you two can KIT: social media, regular FaceTime calls, phone calls, WhatsApp. You can also get creative with it! Maybe you can write letters like pen pals, or send each other postcards with funny pictures. Planning this out will give you both something to look forward to.

* **Plan a fun going away party!** This isn't about saying goodbye. It's about celebrating your friend's new adventure. The days leading up to a big move can be extra stressful, so a party might be a great way to take her mind off it—and remind her how much you care about her.

* **Tell her how you feel.** It's important to stay positive. But you don't want your friend to think you aren't going to miss her like crazy! Reassure her that she means a lot to you and just because she's moving doesn't mean your friendship is over. If you find it hard to express your feelings, you might give a meaningful gift instead, like a framed photo of the two of you to put in her new bedroom.

✳ **Make a post-move plan.** The day your friend leaves is going to be a sad one. Come up with a few self-care activities you can do once she moves away, like journaling, drawing, binge-watching a new TV series, or playing tug-of-war with your dog.

How to Say Goodbye When You're Moving Away

Moving away can feel like the end of the world. No, really—the world as you know it is about to change. You have to say goodbye to your house, your town, your school, and worst of all, your friends.

There's no right way to break this news to your friends. You might want to tell one friend at a time so you can let each of them know how you feel individually. Or you might want to tell the whole group so you can all have a big cry together. You might tell your friends in person, or if you're worried you won't be able to get the words out, you could write all your feelings in a letter, telling them how much you're going to miss them. Ultimately, this is your news, and you get to choose how you're most comfortable sharing it.

Next, don't spend your last weeks together moping around. Plan a few fun activities and make even more great memories to bring with you when you move. You might go to a concert or a sports game together, meet up at your favorite pizza place one last time, or spend the day playing mini golf.

Last but not least, remind your friends (and yourself) that this isn't the end of your friendship. It's just entering a new phase. After you break the news, talk to your friends about all the ways you're going to keep in touch once you're gone. That will help you all realize that this isn't goodbye *forever*. It's goodbye to this era, and hello to the next!

What Kind of Helper Are You?

1. **Your best friend found out the boy she's had a crush on forever asked another girl to the school dance. She's devastated—obviously!—and tells you she's not sure she wants to go to the dance at all now. What do you do?**

   A. Give her a giant hug. And cry. It feels like my heart is broken too!
   B. List all the reasons he doesn't deserve her.
   C. Look up the latest TikTok dance and learn every move with her. If she decides to go to the dance after all, you two can show off your routine.
   D. Make a list of pros and cons with her about the dance so she can decide whether or not she wants to go.

2. **One day after swim team practice, you notice a quiet, shy teammate crying by her locker. When you ask her what's wrong, she admits that another teammate has been body shaming her in the locker room when the coach isn't around. How would you handle it?**

   A. I'd tell her how sorry I am, and that I get it—that same teammate has teased me a few times.
   B. I'd tell her she's beautiful and not to listen to that teammate!
   C. I'd learn everything I can about body shaming so that next practice, I can educate the bullying teammate.
   D. I would go straight to our coach and tell her what's going on.

3. **One of your friends is the understudy to the lead in the school musical. A few days before opening night, the student playing the lead gets sick—so your friend is about to get her turn in spotlight. She's excited at first, but she's also *terrified*. In fact, she admits she's thinking about backing out. "I'm not ready!" she says. What's your reaction?**

A. It's just like when I had to sing the solo at the choir concert last winter. I would tell her I understand how scary that is and that I'll support her no matter what her decision is.

B. Is she kidding? She's, like, *the greatest actress ever.* I'd tell her stage fright is totally normal and I know she's going to be awesome.

C. I would google famous actresses who started as understudies and text the list to her.

D. I'd cancel all my plans and spend the whole afternoon before the musical reading lines with her so she feels more confident.

4. Your school district is opening a second middle school next year. You'll still be attending the same school, but your best friend just found out she has to attend the new one. She's so upset. How do you handle it?

A. This stinks! I'm crying right along with her! And I'll make sure she knows how irreplaceable she is to me as a friend. Next year isn't going to be the same.

B. I try to focus on the bright side. She's not moving away, so we'll still see each other tons outside of school.

C. I will find out everything I can about the new middle school. Maybe they'll have different extracurriculars than our school, like a coding club or a photography class that she'll be into.

D. I'll talk to our principal or email the school board asking if there are any exceptions when it comes to deciding which students will be going to the new campus.

5. A boy in your class shows up wearing *really* expensive sneakers one day. At lunch, a few kids at your table tell you they heard he shoplifted those shoes because there's no way he could've afforded them. You're pretty sure that's not true, and the gossip makes you uncomfortable—especially when you realize the boy overheard their whispers. What would you do?

A. I'd loudly point out that it doesn't mean he stole them. My grandma gave me a really nice necklace for my last birthday. Maybe his sneakers were a gift.

B. I'd smile at him and tell him his shoes look great. Then I'd change the subject so the other kids stop talking about it.

C. I would look the shoes up on my phone. Maybe they were on sale.

D. I'd tell those kids to stop spreading rumors. And if they didn't, I'd report them to a teacher.

6. **Your best friend misses school for a few days because she isn't feeling well. That weekend, you go to her house and learn she was diagnosed with diabetes. She's really sad and overwhelmed by all the changes she's going to have to make in her life. How would you react?**

A. I'd make a pillow fort like we used to do when we were little so we could hide out all weekend and talk until she started to feel better.

B. I'd remind her of the time she broke her leg and how awesome she did in physical therapy afterwards. If she can get through that, she can handle this!

C. I'd research diabetes to learn all about her new lifestyle changes so I can help her prepare.

D. I'd look for a sugar-free recipe alternative for her favorite cookies and bake her a nice big batch.

7. **Your family gave your grandma a new iPad for her birthday. She was excited. But the last time you spoke on the phone, you found out she's having a hard time figuring out how to use FaceTime, and she seems a little embarrassed about it. What would you do?**

A. I'd tell her not to feel bad—maybe there was an update. That throws me off sometimes too.

B. I'd encourage her to try again. In fact, she should hang up the phone and try to FaceTime me right now. She can do this!

C. I'd text her a link to an article with clear, step-by-step instructions on how to use FaceTime.

D. I'd FaceTime her! Maybe once she receives a call, it'll be easier for her to figure out how to make one next time.

Answers

Mostly As: The Empathizer

When someone you love is struggling, you totally feel their pain. You're the first to offer hugs, tissues, and a shoulder to cry on—and your friends and family no doubt love you for it. Just make sure that you check in to see if there's anything else they need too. There might be additional ways you can help out aside from an endless supply of hugs.

Mostly Bs: The Cheerleader

When it comes to offering words of encouragement, you're at the top of the pyramid. Your loved ones know they can come to you when they need a little confidence boost, because you'll be the first to remind them of how great they are. Keep in mind that sometimes, a struggling friend might need to feel sad for a little while. It doesn't mean you failed! Remember that no one feels super peppy 100 percent of the time.

Mostly Cs: The Researcher

A friend's got a problem? Hey, you'll solve it. You get right to work, digging up any information you can to help the two of you figure out how to handle it. And while you're no doubt an A+ problem solver, remember that not all issues can be fixed—but you can definitely use all that data to figure out the best ways to offer support.

Mostly Ds: The Aide

What can I do? That's your first thought when someone needs help. Whether it's quizzing your friend on a subject she's struggling with, cleaning the kitchen while your mom is on a work call, or bringing your bestie ALL the chocolate when her crush breaks her heart, you are one proactive helper! While you're at it, make sure you're truly listening—sometimes, the one thing we need most when we have a problem is someone to hear us out.

ASK THE EXPERT

Cara Goodwin, PhD
Child Psychologist

I am trying to decide what high school I would like to go to next year, when I will be an incoming freshman. It's been very hard for me to please my mom and also choose what school I think is right for me. Any advice?
—Raffy, 14, Connecticut, USA

This is definitely a tough decision! It might be helpful to sit down with your mom and discuss the pros and cons of your different options. Listen to what she says and explain your own feelings clearly. It can help to write down the pros and cons that each person lists on a piece of paper so you can both see them clearly. Make sure you are writing down every pro and con. Even if you don't agree with each other's opinion, you'll both feel heard and understood. Once you have written down each pro and con, take a day or two to think things over. Then explain your decision clearly to your mom using the lists to back up your thoughts. Give her a chance to explain her opinion. If you follow these steps, you should be able to reach an outcome you're both happy with. Finally, agree on a time that you will revisit the decision if either of you feel like it isn't working out.

Learning to regulate your emotions is a lifelong process, so it is more than okay that you don't have it down yet. There are some ways you can practice this important skill, though. The first step is learning to identify and name your feelings. When you feel "off," try to figure out whether you feel sad, angry, anxious, disappointed, or another emotion. Then try to identify signs in your body that you are feeling that emotion, such as a racing heart. Noticing signs like this can help you pinpoint the emotion when it comes up again. Start using coping strategies that work for you. Different coping strategies work for different people, so the only way to know if they work is to try them out. Some strategies include deep breathing, listening to music, thinking about the situation in a different way, talking to yourself in a different way (like telling yourself you can do it when your brain is telling you that you can't), going for a walk, or talking to a friend or family member. It is also important to remember that taking care of yourself will make emotional regulation easier—so make sure you are getting enough sleep, eating regular meals, and taking time to relax. If learning to regulate your emotions seems particularly hard for you, don't hesitate to seek help from a mental health professional, such as a psychologist or therapist.

CHAPTER 6

YOU'VE GOT THIS!

That's enough doom and gloom! We talked about a ton of "downs"—now let's focus on the "ups." You're making new friends and trying fun new things. You aren't afraid to ask for help, and you're comfortable saying no. When the punches come, you know how to roll with them.

In other words, you might get anxious sometimes, but that's not stopping you from having a social life. And with that comes all kinds of exciting

opportunities, because people will no doubt notice what a cool, confident Rebel Girl you're becoming. Bravery is exponential—with every brave choice you make, your next chance to be brave gets a little bit easier!

Don't be surprised if you're soon considering things that you never would have done in the past. You might want to sign up to be a mentor. Start your own volunteer group. Speak to local reporters about issues in your community or at your school. The sky's the limit—and no matter what happens, you've got this.

HOW TO BECOME A STRONG PUBLIC SPEAKER

The flyer appears out of nowhere one morning. Interested in running for Student Council? And now you can't stop thinking about it. You have so many ideas on how to improve your school. Plus, your friends would be so supportive—you can already imagine how helpful they'll be with your campaign.

But all the candidates have to make a speech. In front of the *whole student body*.

Take a deep breath. You can totally do this. We often assume that good public speakers are just born that way. And it's true that some people are naturally charismatic and love being in the spotlight. But you know what else is true?

REBEL GIRLS 4 PRESIDENT

Anyone can learn to be a strong public speaker. Even if the thought of standing up in front of your peers makes your knees turn to jelly.

And here's a little secret. Those amazing public speakers you admire? *They get nervous too!* Nerves are totally normal when all eyes are on you. The trick is channeling that nervous energy into your words so everyone can see how passionate you are. Next time you have to give a speech, try the following tips:

* **Write an outline *and* a full speech.** You might hear advice to work only with an outline, because if you're reading from a script, you risk sounding stiff and awkward. But writing out your speech word for word will help you figure out exactly how you want to phrase everything.

* **Practice, practice, practice!** Start by reading your script—yes, right off the page! Yes, even if you sound stiff and awkward. Your goal isn't to memorize every word, but to get a feel for the flow of your speech.

* **Use your outline.** Once you're comfortable reading the script, set it aside and try delivering the speech using only your outline. Remember, this was never about memorizing every word. You're going to change a few phrases, skip a sentence or two—you might even ad-lib something new! The key is to keep going, no matter what. No run-through of your speech is going to be perfect, but that's not what you're aiming for. With every performance, you're going to sound a little more natural and feel a little more confident.

* **Find an audience.** A small one to start with. This might be a few friends, a parent, or a sibling—anyone you know you can count on to offer encouragement. Each time you deliver your speech, try to make a little more eye contact with your audience. At first, it might feel scary to take your eyes off your outline, but you'll get more used to it with every round.

* **Prepare the night before the speech.** Lay out what you're going to wear, and choose something you feel comfortable and confident in. Decide what you're going to eat (never give a speech on an empty stomach!) and choose foods you know don't upset your stomach. Before you leave, don't forget to do your superhero pose!

* **Bring your script and your outline.** Yes, the goal is to use your outline during your speech. But simply having your full script right there with you will ease your nerves. If you totally blank out, your words are within reach.

* **Remember that the audience is on your side.** Sometimes, we convince ourselves that everyone watching wants us to fail. But of course, that's not true. Your peers want you to hit this out of the park, so take a nice deep breath, smile, and have fun!

WHAT THE REBELS SAY

"Get out there and have fun, even if you're scared."
—Ellie, 11, California, USA

Bonus Tips for Class Presentations

Giving a presentation in front of your whole class is a great opportunity to practice those public speaking skills. Here are a few more tips to help make your presentation shine:

✳ *Include humor or personal anecdotes.* Of course, you want to make sure they're appropriate for school—not to mention relevant to your presentation topic. But getting your classmates and teachers to laugh, especially near the beginning of your presentation, is a great way to break the ice and help you relax.

* *Speak clearly and monitor your speed.* When we're nervous, we start to mumble. Sometimes, we talk at top speed, or if we're reading, we might go extra slow. When you practice, make sure you're working on a calm, clear delivery at an easy-to-understand pace.

* *Include visual and audio aids.* This might include video or sound clips, a slide show, a poster board with data you've collected, charts, graphs, or anything that can enhance your presentation. The best part? All those eyes will be on your cool displays instead of you!

* *Get creative!* You can follow instructions while still having a little fun and adding a personal touch to your presentation. If you're in doubt about that little something extra you're thinking of including, run it by your teacher first.

* *Make it interactive.* Asking your classmates questions, or inviting them to ask you questions, can open things up and help take the pressure off of you. Plus, it's a great way to make sure everyone stays engaged.

HOW TO BE A LEADER

Anyone can be a leader—including you! It doesn't matter if you're an introvert or an extrovert, shy or outspoken, super anxious or rarely nervous at all. It's easy to think that a leader is simply the person who takes charge of a situation and tells others what to do. But the truth is, leadership is much more complex than that. A truly great leader doesn't necessarily command others to do good things. They *inspire* others to do good things.

* **Leaders listen.** When you're passionate about a cause, it's natural to talk about it. But make sure you're hearing ideas and concerns from those around you too.

* **Leaders believe.** Do you believe you can create a positive change in the world? You should! And when you do, you'll inspire others to do the same.

* **Leaders organize.** If you want something done, don't wait for someone else to come up with a plan. You don't need permission to start organizing.

* **Leaders problem-solve.** No matter what you're trying to achieve, you're probably going to run into a few obstacles. Don't give up! Think it through and come up with a way to overcome the issue and keep going. Perhaps you've heard that a local animal shelter is running low on supplies. You want to help. So you put your problem-solving and leadership skills to work by organizing a bake sale to raise money to buy more supplies.

* **Leaders speak truth.** The best leaders are able to set their egos aside. That means admitting when you've made a mistake, as well as listening to advice and criticism from others.

If you're interested in developing your leadership skills, talk to your school administration or local community centers about teen leadership classes and activities.

Picture This

Dominique loves school. She plays trombone in a band, her favorite class is social studies, and she and her closest friends are all in the debate club. But as much as she loves her school, she has been noticing some issues. Like that day her friend

Cristin got sent home for violating the dress code with a skirt that was too short. But Dominique can't help thinking Cristin's skirt was longer than the cheerleaders' uniforms! How is that fair?

Then there was that time the school held a canned food drive. But hardly anyone brought donations because no one knew about it. The principal mentioned it once or twice during announcements, but Dominique thinks there should have been flyers everywhere—and notices for kids to take home to their parents.

The biggest problem is the bullying. There are rarely teachers in the hall near the vending machines after lunch, and a few kids have been hanging out there, tripping anyone who passes by and then demanding they hand over change for the vending machine.

When the newspaper staff teacher tells them the next issue will include a call for students interested in running for student council, Dominique starts to think about what she would do as class president. But there's no way she's going to run. She'd have to campaign and make speeches, and she has never really wanted that kind of spotlight.

She mentions this to her friends, who beg her to run.

"You have so many great ideas, Dominique," Cristin says. "You could make such a difference!"

Dominique's stomach flutters with nerves—but also excitement. She decides to run, and her friends eagerly help her by coming up with a slogan, making posters, and designing flyers to hand out. Dominique spends weeks working on a speech that covers all of the issues she has noticed, as well as solutions she would implement as president. She practices every day in front of her friends and family until she feels prepared.

The speech goes great! Dominique makes a few mistakes, but she recovers quickly. Afterwards, dozens of students she doesn't even know come up to her to say how much they appreciate her talking about those issues.

"I got sent home for violating dress code, but my friend didn't—and we were wearing the same top," one girl says.

"I'm not too scared to walk past the vending machines anymore," another boy tells her. "I'm really glad you brought that up."

When the votes come in, Dominique wins! She's thrilled—and looking back, she can't believe she almost didn't run. Now she can turn all her ideas into reality and make her school an even better place.

Journal Prompts on Leadership

Journaling can be a a powerful tool. The act of writing down our thoughts allows us to identify our fears, worries, hopes, and dreams, and helps us get clear on what we want—and how we're going to get it.

Turn any notebook into a leadership journal. Jot down your answers to these questions and prompts, and reflect on what being a leader means to you.

* What are the qualities of a great leader?
* Name three leaders (in any field) you admire, and why.
* Write about a recent incident where you showed excellent leadership.
* What do you think is the biggest challenge of being a leader, and why?
* What do you think is the best way to earn someone's respect?
* What do you think is the best way to earn someone's trust?
* Write about a time when someone you know showed leadership through actions instead of words.
* What is the difference between being a leader and being popular?
* Write about an influencer who is also a great leader, and why.
* Write about an influencer who is NOT a good leader, and why.

140

How to Be an Ally to Marginalized Groups

You've already learned about being inclusive when it comes to making new friends. A huge part of inclusivity is being curious about other cultures and celebrating individuality. Because we're all different! And many of us belong to one or more marginalized groups.

What's a marginalized group? It's a group of people with shared traits who are ostracized, treated differently, discriminated against, or disempowered by society. They might be marginalized based on:

* gender identity
* sexual orientation
* disability
* ethnicity
* skin color
* socio-economic status
* religion
* size
* age
* mental health

If you belong to a marginalized group, you already understand the specific types of injustices that group deals with. Perhaps you're already an advocate for change! Those injustices will look and feel different from one group to another. That's why the most important thing you can do as an ally to *all* marginalized groups is to listen when they talk about the specific injustices they experience. The more you learn about what others have to deal

WHAT THE REBELS SAY

"My story is a freedom song of struggle. It is about finding one's purpose, how to overcome fear and stand up for causes bigger than one's self."
—Coretta Scott King, activist and author

with, the better prepared you'll be to advocate for them. As you listen and learn, put the following practices into place.

* **Look for real-life examples.** If you've never experienced a specific type of micro-aggression—for example, one based on the color of your skin—you may not have noticed them before. Once you learn about it, pay attention! The more you discover about the experiences of other marginalized groups, the more you'll start to notice them.

* **Speak up.** If you do see or hear someone demonstrating prejudice, let them know what you've learned. The best way to do this is calmly and with kindness. Using an aggressive tone or harsh words is rarely effective when you're trying to help. After all, there was a time when you didn't know this, either. Speaking of . . .

* **Avoid being defensive.** If you suddenly find out you've been using a word that is considered offensive to a community, you might feel guilty—or even defensive. After all, you didn't know! And that's okay. But now, you *do* know. The important thing is what you do next.

* **Do your own research.** It isn't a marginalized person's job to educate everyone about the type of injustice they deal with on a daily basis. Take it upon yourself to research independently. There are tons of activists from all kinds of marginalized communities who share free resources online.

* **Stand up.** If you witness a marginalized person experiencing hate, let them know you're on their side. Whether you should intervene in the moment depends on your safety. If there is any threat of violence, it's best to notify the nearest adult immediately. If you do feel safe inserting yourself into the situation, focus on offering the victim support and comfort instead of lashing out at the attacker.

WHAT TO DO WHEN THE NEWS MAKES YOU UPSET

You woke up in a pretty good mood. But when you open your phone, the first thing you see is a viral news story about something terrible that happened. And that good mood spirals *fast*. Now you're scared and sad and wondering if you can spend the day in bed.

Sometimes, it feels like we're drowning in a sea of never-ending bad news. It can make us feel like the world is a dangerous and awful place. And that makes us feel unsafe. Social media plays a huge role in how we share news. Think about it—before the Internet was around, people relied on daily newspapers

and broadcasts to find out what was happening all over the world. Now, we can pretty much find up-to-the-minute information about anything, anytime. It's a *lot*. So, it's up to us to manage our behaviors in a way that helps us stay informed while taking care of our mental health. Here are a few strategies you can try when the news makes you upset:

* **Create your own "news windows."** That means setting aside a specific time of day to catch up on the news, and picking sites meant for kids, like BBC Newsround or TIME for Kids. If seeing bad news in the morning sets you up to have a bad day, try checking it during lunch instead. If reading the news at night keeps you tossing and turning with anxiety, maybe move your news window to right after school.

* **Use social media filters.** Pretty much every social media app allows you to block posts from specific sources or that use certain hashtags. Flip them on when you want to scroll through posts without getting hit with news stories.

* **Seek out good news.** News outlets often highlight the scariest or saddest events in the world. But there are lots of outlets and newsletters out there that focus on sharing all of the positive things happening too. Subscribe, follow, and strike your own balance when it comes to the news you consume.

* **Get offline regularly.** Put your phone away for a little while and take a break from the news. Going on a bike ride, playing basketball with your friends, having a board game night, or going on a walk through your neighborhood will help bring down your stress levels.

* **Take action.** Sometimes, the best way to react to a bad news story is to figure out how you can help. Was there a tornado the next town over? Look for opportunities to volunteer or donate items to victims. Whether it's joining a protest or march, sharing helpful resources on your socials, or signing petitions, taking action will ease your anxiety and give you something positive to focus on.

15 Ways to Make a Difference in Your Community

Try these simple but impactful ways to give back.

* Donate old toys and clothes to a local charity.
* Volunteer at a shelter or food pantry.
* Join a park or beach cleanup.
* Help out at your local library's book drive.
* Call your city council members to make your voice heard on local issues.
* Attend school board meetings.
* Take a first aid or CPR class.
* Participate in Earth Day activities.
* Write postcards to military personnel overseas.
* Help out in your local community garden.
* Offer to help elderly neighbors with chores.
* Talk to your parents and friends about carpooling.
* Sign up to be a tutor or mentor.
* Use cloth bags when you shop.
* Stop to pick up and throw away litter.

What Positive Changes Can You Make?

1. **Every year, there's a field trip, and it's always different. What are you hoping the trip will be this year?**

   A. The aquarium
   B. The nature reserve
   C. The amusement park
   D. A tour of town hall

2. **Which of the following amazing Rebel Girls do you most want to be like?**

   A. Genesis Butler, animal rights activist and one of the youngest TEDx speakers ever.
   B. Greta Thunberg, environmental activist who addressed the United Nations Climate Change Conference.
   C. Marley Dias, author and founder of #1000BlackGirlBooks.
   D. Kenidra Woods, organizer of the National Rally for Peace in response to gun violence in her community.

3. **You're applying for a scholarship that requires 20 hours of community service with one of the following options. Which one is your first choice?**

   A. Helping a rescue organization for stray cats.
   B. Joining a cleanup crew at the local park.
   C. Visiting the local retirement center.
   D. Volunteering at the local farmer's market.

4. **Your family is going to make a big donation to a charity. Which one do you want to choose?**

   A. Best Friends Animal Society
   B. Rainforest Alliance
   C. Save the Children
   D. A local nonprofit organization that focuses on improving our community

5. **Which of the following quotes resonates with you the most?**

    A. "You cannot share your life with a dog or a cat and not know perfectly well that animals have personalities and minds and feelings." —Jane Goodall

    B. "We are on Earth to take care of life. We are on Earth to take care of each other." —Xiye Bastida

    C. "I don't believe you can stand for freedom for one group of people and deny it to others." —Coretta Scott King

    D. "Love too often gets buried in a world of hurt and fear. And we have to work to dig it out so we can share it with our family, our friends, and our neighbors." —Dolly Parton

6. **Think about all the different accounts you follow on social media. If you had to categorize them, the biggest category would probably be . . .**

    A. Adorable pets.
    B. Amazing places all over the globe.
    C. Selfies!
    D. Friends, family, and cool stuff in my community.

7. **The news is stressing you out. Time to put your phone away and unwind. What's your go-to destressing activity?**

    A. Taking my dog to the park for a game of fetch.
    B. Grabbing my bike and taking a ride on a local trail through the woods.
    C. Getting rowdy with my friends at a soccer match.
    D. Visiting my local library, then finding a bench so I can sit outside and read.

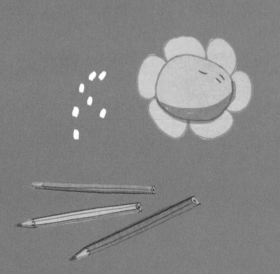

Answers

Mostly As: Animal Activism

You're passionate about all creatures, great and small. Your local animal shelter might have volunteer opportunities where you can walk, feed, and play with cats and dogs. You might even consider fostering or adopting one yourself. Another option is to check out any wildlife conservation programs in your area. Whether you live near the water, in the mountains, close to swamplands or even a desert, there's tons of diverse wildlife in your state—and conservation groups dedicated to helping them thrive.

Mostly Bs: Planet Protection

Melting glaciers, rising temperatures, extreme weather—you know climate change is a huge issue, and you're determined to do what you can to help. You might try looking for a conservation group that tackles things like cleaning up nature trails, parks, or beaches and other waterfront areas. If you live near farmland, many farmers are happy to take on volunteers to assist with harvesting and packaging fruits and vegetables. Another option is an environmental program for kids that takes political actions such as organizing protests and contacting government officials.

Mostly Cs: Social Service

You're a people person! When you see someone in need, you can't rest until you've figured out how to help. Youth clubs, Scout groups, and local seasonal camps are all great programs with volunteer opportunities. You might visit nursing homes or children's hospitals to visit with patients. Your community might have various shelters for unhoused people, migrants and refugees, and victims of natural disasters, as well as soup kitchens and food banks, all of which need caring kids like you to lend a helping hand.

Mostly Ds: Community Champion

You know exactly what makes your community special, and you're super proud to live here. Check with your local community center, tourism board, or center for the arts to ask about upcoming events, festivals, or sports games that are in need of volunteers. If there's a local business like a bookshop, boutique, or bakery that you love, talk to the managers about how you can help spread the word.

ASK THE EXPERT

Cara Goodwin, PhD
Child Psychologist

My Girl Scout troop is doing an overnight at the mall. Do you have any tips to calm my nerves about being away from my family?
—Cassie, 10, Maryland, USA

An overnight trip can be both exciting and nerve-racking. When you're thinking about the sleepover, try focusing on the fun and positive parts of it. It can help to remember why you wanted to go on the trip in the first place. Maybe you were excited to spend more time with your troop, or to try something new. You may still miss your family and that is okay too. Make a plan for what to do when you're feeling homesick, like talking to a trusted friend or reminding yourself of something fun you're going to do with them when you get home. It may be tempting to decide not to go on the Girl Scout trip because you're nervous, but giving in to your anxiety will only make these types of trips even harder in the future.

How often should I try new things? Is it normal to not like new things?
—Neva, 11, California, USA

It is *so* normal to have difficulty trying new things. Most people don't like uncertainty and unpredictability. It is so much easier to stay in our routine and stick to what we know. It is hard to say exactly how often you should be trying new things, because it really depends on what feels right for you. However, I would challenge you to think of all the benefits that trying new things could bring to your life, such as making new friends, discovering new passions, and becoming a braver and more outgoing person. Perhaps set a goal for yourself to try something new once a month—even small things like a different ice cream flavor! This can help you realize that trying new things is often fun as opposed to scary.

RESOURCES

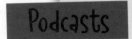

Books

All Things Friendship by Sara Jin Li and Camila Rivera
BFF or NRF (Not Really Friends) by Jessica Speer
The Confidence Code for Girls by Katty Kay and Claire Shipman
Growing Up Powerful by Nona Willis Aronowitz
Growing Up Powerful Journal by Nona Willis Aronowitz
Mindful Me by Whitney Stewart
Outsmarting Worry by Dawn Huebner
What Can I Say? By Catherine Newman

Podcasts

10 for Tweens + Teens
A Kids Book About: The Podcast
Mostly Mindful for Teens and Tweens
Rebel Girls Growing Up Powerful Podcast
Tai Asks Why?
This Teenage Life

Websites

Anxiety in the Classroom | anxietyintheclassroom.org/student
Childline | childline.org.uk
Girls' Life | girlslife.com
Miss O and Friends | missoandfriends.com
Nemours KidsHealth | kidshealth.org/en/kids
StopBullying | stopbullying.gov/kids
Your Life Your Voice | yourlifeyourvoice.org

And Two For Your Parents . . .

Book

This Is So Awkward: Modern Puberty Explained
by Cara Natterson and Vanessa Kroll Bennett

Podcast

Dear Highlights Podcast

MEET THE CREATORS

MICHELLE SCHUSTERMAN is the author of more than 20 critically acclaimed novels for middle grade and young adult readers. Her books have received starred reviews from *Kirkus Reviews*, *Booklist*, and *Publishers Weekly*, as well as honors including multiple Junior Library Guild selections, the CBCC Best of 2019 List, ALA's Rainbow List and Quick Picks for Reluctant Readers List, and the NC State College of Education Comic Relief Reading List. Michelle is also a developmental editor at Dovetail Fiction, the young adult imprint of the book packager Working Partners. Michelle can be found roaming mountains, deserts, and beaches in a van camper with her husband and their Labrador, Rosa.

CARA GOODWIN, PhD, is the founder of Parenting Translator, a best-selling author, and a licensed psychologist with a PhD in child clinical psychology. She is also a mother to four young children. As a psychologist, she specializes in taking the most recent scientific findings and "translating" them into information that parents, caregivers, and children can use in their everyday lives. She started Parenting Translator in order to provide families with information that is is helpful, relevant, and accurate for parents and based in research. Cara has a bachelor's degree in psychology and neuroscience from the University of Virginia, a master's in developmental psychiatry from Cambridge University, a master's in child psychology from Vanderbilt University, and a PhD in child psychology from the University of North Carolina at Chapel Hill. You can visit her website at www.parentingtranslator.com, follow her on Instagram @parentingtranslator, or subscribe to her Substack at parentingtranslator.substack.com.

Julia Christians Hey there, I'm Julia, a spirited children's book illustrator from the heart of Germany. With a diploma in Communications Design from the University of Art in Brunswick (Class of 2011), I've been crafting colorful worlds since day one. Since 2018, I've been on a wild ride as a freelance illustrator, bringing characters to life and painting stories that leap off the page. I call the deep, mysterious embrace of the Harz Mountains home, where my lively crew includes a loving husband, a pack of giggling kids, and a handful of mischievous dogs.

When I'm not wielding my trusty paintbrush, I'm out exploring the secrets of the forest, finding inspiration in every rustle and whisper. My illustrations are all about sparking wonder and inviting young minds to embark on captivating adventures.

So, jump into my world of illustrations, where each stroke is a ticket to a land of imagination, and every page is an invitation to dance with creativity.

READ MORE BOOKS!

Let the stories of real-life women and girls entertain and inspire you. Each volume in the Good Night Stories series includes 100 tales of extraordinary women.

Check out these mini books too! Each one contains 25 tales of talented women, along with engaging activities.

Filled with helpful advice, Q&As between experts and girls around the world, and fun quizzes, *Growing Up Powerful* has the inside scoop on all things girlhood and helps tweens and teens become their most confident selves.

This bold, big-hearted series gives girls the tools they need to communicate clearly, calm their worries, and thrive in the world today.

In *Dear Rebel*, 145 extraordinary teens and women share their best advice for the girls of today. Through letters, poems, essays, self-portraits, and more, they tackle topics like overcoming obstacles, discovering your passions, and dreaming big.

Dig deeper into the lives of five real-life heroines with the Rebel Girls chapter book series.

Uncover the groundbreaking inventions of Ada Lovelace, one of the world's first computer programmers.

Learn the exciting business of Madam C.J. Walker, the hair care industry pioneer and first female self-made millionaire in the US.

Explore the thrilling adventures of Junko Tabei, the first female climber to summit Mount Everest.

Discover the inspiring story of Dr. Wangari Maathai, the Nobel Peace Prize–winning environmental activist from Kenya.

Follow the awe-inspiring career of Alicia Alonso, a world-renowned prima ballerina from Cuba.

The Rebel Girls Handbook is the ultimate collection of facts, trivia, and imaginative activities about 300+ world-changing women and girls.

The quirky questions in these books help curious readers explore their personalities, forecast their futures, and find common ground with extraordinary women who've come before them. Plus, they're tons of fun!

AUDIO ADVENTURES

The Rebel Girls podcast is packed with exciting stories of women and girls from around the world and throughout history. They've raised their voices, broken boundaries, and changed the world for the better.

Download the Rebel Girls app to listen to even more Rebel Girls stories. Filled with the adventures and accomplishments of women, the Rebel Girls app is designed to entertain, inspire, and build confidence in listeners everywhere.

For more confidence-boosting content, don't miss the Growing Up Powerful podcast, available on the Rebel Girls app or wherever you listen to podcasts.

ABOUT REBEL GIRLS

REBEL GIRLS, a certified B Corporation, is a global, multi-platform empowerment brand dedicated to helping raise the most inspired and confident generation of girls through content, experiences, products, and community. Originating from an international best-selling children's book, Rebel Girls amplifies stories of real-life, extraordinary women throughout history, geography, and field of excellence. With a growing community of 30 million self-identified Rebel Girls spanning more than 100 countries, the brand engages with Generation Alpha through its book series, premier app and audio content, events, and merchandise. To date, Rebel Girls has sold more than 11 million books in 50 languages and reached 40 million audio listens. Award recognition includes the *New York Times* bestseller list, the 2022 Apple Design Award for Social Impact, multiple Webby Awards for Family & Kids and Education, and Common Sense Media Selection honors, among others.

As a B Corp, we're part of a global community of businesses that meet high standards of social and environmental impact.

Join the Rebel Girls Community!

Visit rebelgirls.com and sign up for our email list to find exclusive sneak peeks, promos, activities, and more. You can also email us at hello@rebelgirls.com.

- ✦ **YouTube:** youtube.com/rebelgirls
- ✦ **App:** rebelgirls.com/audio
- ✦ **Podcast:** rebelgirls.com/podcast
- ✦ **Facebook:** facebook.com/rebelgirls
- ✦ **Instagram:** @rebelgirls
- ✦ **Email:** hello@rebelgirls.com
- ✦ **Web:** rebelgirls.com

If you liked this book, please take a moment to review it wherever you prefer!